Words and Witness

Words and Witness

Narrative and Aesthetic Strategies in the Representation of the Holocaust

Lea Wernick Fridman

State University of New York Press

Published by
State University of New York Press, Albany

For information, address State University of New York Press,
State University Plaza, Albany, N.Y. 12246

Production by Michael Haggett
Marketing by Dana E. Yanulavich

Library of Congress Cataloging-in-Publication Data

Fridman, Lea Wernick, 1949–
    Words and witness : narrative and aesthetic strategies in the
representation of the Holocaust / Lea Wernick Fridman.
        p.   cm.
    Includes bibliographical references and index.
    ISBN 0-7914-4609-3 (HC : acid free). — ISBN 0-7914-4610-7 (PB :
acid free)
    1. Holocaust, Jewish (1939–1945), in literature. I. Title.
PN56.H55F75 2000
809´.93358—dc21
                                                          99-42869
                                                             CIP

10 9 8 7 6 5 4 3 2 1

For my children,
      Shaoul, Shoshana, Ruthie
      Michal, Moshe, and Abie

And for my granddaughters,
      Chava and Hadassa

. . . but I have a voice too and for good or evil mine is the speech that cannot be silenced.

Joseph Conrad

My corner of Europe, owing to the extraordinary and lethal events that have been occurring there, comparable only to violent earthquakes, affords a peculiar perspective. As a result, all of us who come from those parts appraise poetry slightly different than do the majority of my audience, for we tend to view it as a witness and participant in one of mankind's major transformations.

Czeslaw Milosz

Contents

Acknowledgments

I wish to acknowledge two institutes that supported work on this manuscript in its fledgling days, the American Association for University Women and the Jack P. Eisner Institute of Holocaust Studies. This book was made possible by the support these foundations gave me at early stages of its writing.

There are many other kinds of debt one owes in an undertaking of this sort. There are debts to those who paved the way, those who served as example, those who gave practical assistance, those who gave moral and morale assistance, and those who bore, with love and patience, the demands of such a project.

Geoffrey Hartman deserves acknowledgment of the first sort. The Holocaust did not emerge as an important subject of study in American literary and intellectual circles because it was deserving of such study. It emerged as an important subject of study because some thinkers were, at a certain point in time, willing to go a less popular professional route, to insist on the centrality of the subject in their work and in their thinking. Integrity, wherever it plays a role in a discipline or in the life of a community, cannot be overvalued.

It is with great affection and admiration that I thank Rosette Lamont for the example of her commitment to the life of the mind and the panache with which she lives her commitment. Her presence is everywhere in these pages, although I am fully responsible for any and all errors of fact and judgment.

The early days of Holocaust study and conferences were days in which a shared sense of breaking ground and of moral engagement made this work bearable. One's professional community was also a community of conscience. My shelves are filled with the books of these writers and friends who were part of this circuit and who engaged, early on, with difficult questions and difficult materials. Herman Rapaport, Angelika Rauch, Terrence Des Pres, Richard Weisberg, Alvin Rosenfeld, Lawrence Langer, Sidra Ezrahi, Tony Brinkley, Steven Joura, Sarah Horowitz, Ellen Fine, Peter Balakian, Carolyn Forché, Sandor Goodheart, Susan Shapiro, Sabina Goetz, Jim Hatley, Frieda Aron, Jane Gerber, Saul Friedlander, Elie Wiesel, Geoffrey Hartman, Robert Lifton, Aharon Appelfeld, and Cynthia Ozick are only some of the earlier, mostly literary folks, whose paths crossed mine.

Never underestimate the practical. I am touched by the generosity of friends who happily read my manuscript, encouraged, critiqued, and caught editorial blemishes. Herman Rapaport's encouragement and comments were invaluable to me. Carolla Sautter, Clara Freeman, Stanley Babin, Michael Denbo, Inez Martinez, Isidor Apterbach, Kryssa Schemmerling, Louise Jaffe, Curt Olsen, and Sharona Levy all read different pieces of this manuscript at various stages. My editors at SUNY Press, James Peltz and Michael Haggett, were available and ever patient with my questions. I thank them and the entire staff at SUNY. And I thank Judy Protus, James McPherson, Nancy Price, and Erich Wirth for their additional editorial help.

Not all paths are smooth. There are no words sufficient to thank Stanley Babin, Vera Gruber, Susan Aranoff, Akiva Kaminsky, Clara Freeman, Joelle Wallach, Sharona Levy, Judith Wilde, Edith Everett, Reuben Fridman, and Stephen Weidenborner for the consistent support they provided during a long and rocky period of my life.

A serious intellectual or artistic life places large demands on the spirit, on attention, and on time. My children have borne my commitments with grace and with deep love. They make this difficult world also beautiful.

I would also like to acknowledge the following publishers for their kind permission to reprint from their works:

Jean-François Lyotard, *The Differend: Phrases in Dispute*, translated by Georges Van Den Abbeele (University of Minnesota Press, 1988). Originally published as *Le Différend*, copyright 1983 by Les Éditions de Minuit.

Excerpts from *Badenheim 1939* by Aharon Apelfeld, Dalya Bilyu, translator. Reprinted by permission of David R. Godine, Publisher, Inc. Copyright 1980 by Aharon Appelfeld, Dalya Bilyu, translator.

Exerpts from *Night* by Elie Wiesel, translated by Stella Rodway. Copyright 1960 by MacGibbon and Kee. Copyright renewed 1988 by the Collins Publishing Company. Reprinted by permission of Hill and Wang, a division of Farrar, Straus, & Giroux, Inc.

Excerpts from *Heart of Darkness: A Norton Critical Edition, Third Edition*. Joseph Conrad, edited by Robert Kimbrough. Copyright 1988, 1971, 1963 by W. W. Norton & Company, Inc. Reprinted by permission of W. W. Norton & Company, Inc.

Excerpts from *The Witness of Poetry* by Czeslaw Miloscz. Copyright 1983 by the President and Fellows of Harvard College. Reprinted by permission of Harvard University Press.

"With a Variable Key" by Paul Celan from *Poems of Paul Celan*, translated by Michael Hamburger. Translation copyright 1972, 1980, 1988, 1995 by Michael Hamburger. Reprinted by permission of Persea Books, Inc. (New York).

Introduction

It was clear to me from the outset of this study that the traumatic historical event constitutes a special category of difficulty with respect to artistic expression. The more I read across a range of genres, the more I realized how profoundly this difficulty shapes narrative, descriptive, and poetic attempts to represent what I have called "historical horror." I am fascinated by the boundary separating the representable from the unrepresentable and by my sense that works on either side of this boundary are governed by a decidedly different dynamic and set of rules from one another. It is my assumption and the assumption of this study that where we cannot represent, we must study the "rules" of non-representing in the attempt to gain access to "unrepresentability." The work at hand makes only a modest gesture at laying bare such a set of rules, but such implications are not accidental to this study.

The original intent of this study was to uncover a set of relations among a large number of works of "historical horror" in different genres and languages, to show that these works of film and poetry, of fictional narrative, of memoir, and of testimony, are related on formal as well as on thematic grounds. I wanted to show how novels in Italian by Elsa Morante and in Dutch by Harry Mulisch stood on the same writerly decisions and struggles as the Yiddish poems of Sutzkever, the Hebrew short stories of Ida Fink, and the Polish stories of Tadeusz Borowski. I wanted to uncover the necessary connections between the experience of historical trauma and its expression and in so doing, to uncover a formal coherence among a diverse group of works of "historical horror." I set up my first chapter with the goal in mind of clarifying this notion of "historical horror."

Almost without thinking, I reached for Joseph Conrad's *Heart of Darkness*. I hoped by contrasting the literary and gothic horror of Poe with the literary but historical horror of Conrad, to see each one more clearly and thus gain a handle on the issues involved in works of historical horror. The comparison proved more powerful than I had suspected, and I came to marvel at the ease with which the word "horror" is used to refer to such distinct orders of experience and expression. Conrad's great novella speaks pointedly to every question raised by traumatic historical utterance—there is no paradox, no recognition that Conrad fails to raise. As I compared *Heart of Darkness* to other works representing historical horror, it became more confirmed in my thinking as a paradigm of literary motifs, devices, and structures that are constitutive of representations of historical horror.

Thus my first chapter presents *Heart of Darkness* as a model of literary strategies in the representation of historical horror. In the chapters that follow, I extrapolate from features and strategies of "historical horror" as they appear in that novella, to identical strategies found in literary representations of the Holocaust. My opening chapter provides an analysis of formal issues that explain these similarities. Hence this chapter, "History, Fantasy, and Horror," contrasts the treatment of silence and of the real in Poe and in Conrad and concludes that both are constitutive elements of traumatic utterance.

The chapters that follow examine works of Holocaust fiction, film, memoir, and poetry in exactly these terms. Chapters 2 and 3 are devoted to a consideration of silence in poetry, film, and fiction dealing with the Holocaust. Chapters 4 and 5 examine the problematic of disbelief that accompanies events of horror and makes their "realness" an issue in formal ways. In all of these chapters I am interested in the fluid and yet determined relations between an experience and the form it takes, in the signal ways that narrative and description manage to tell in the very act of avoiding the telling.

At least in literary terms, I emerge from my study of works by Aharon Appelfeld, by Dan Pagis, by Piotr Rawicz, by Claude Lanzmann, by Charlotte Delbo, and others with a deepened appreciation of "voice." Where words do not suffice, the burden of communication shifts onto voice. Viewed in this light, it would be instructive to reread Conrad, his presentation of Kurtz as a voice, his substitution of voice for words, detail, and description as the means by which the unrepresentable is then communicated to Marlow and through Marlow to society. The literature of "historical horror" privileges the voiced dimension of literary expression and requires us to read, or better, to experience a flow of words with an acute and musical ear. It is my hope that the readings offered will point the reader in this direction.

At the same time I am more deeply convinced of an existential connection between the experience of historical trauma and its utterance in poetic and literary form. It is precisely in the manner of expression, in the rhetorical and other strategies deployed by the writer in his effort to represent such material, that we can trace the existential mark of an event. Jean-François Lyotard writes of "the differend:"

> This state is signaled by what one ordinarily calls a feeling: "One cannot find the words," etc. A lot of searching must be done to find new rules for forming and linking phrases that are able to express the differend disclosed by the feeling. . . . What is at stake in a literature, in a philosophy, in a politics perhaps, is to bear witness to differends by finding idioms for them.[1]

My first interest in this study has been to identify and explore those idioms.

Much literary criticism of Holocaust writing turns into writing about history and about horror in history. In my view, it is the job of the work of art to bring illumination to a particular corner of human experience, and it is the job of the critic to illuminate the illumination, to comment on art and not on life. The best literary essays on Holocaust works seem to follow this rule: they focus a trained sensibility and the skills of disciplined comment on a work of art. The critic functions, in relation to a work of art, like a fine pianist who, in the performance itself, discovers a world of subtle relationships amongst different voices and elements of a piece of music, an awareness of which enters into that performance and brings the listener (or reader) a fuller experience of a musical composition. There is a natural conspiracy here of the artist and the critic to cast light on the appalling, the confounding, but also on the miraculous in human experience. Perhaps there is a bit of miracle, too, in that partnering.

Chapter 1

History, Fantasy, and Horror

> Horror is a shock, a time of utter blindness.
>
> —*Milan Kundera*

The twentieth century was marked by catastrophe and by large-scale political violence as no other one before it. When I ask my Brooklyn students to write about the ways in which political violence has affected their families, there is rarely a student who is lacking in rich materials for the assignment. Catastrophe throws lives and social relations—all patterns of normal living—into disarray. More subtly, but with profound and wide-ranging implications, catastrophe subverts the very conventions and understandings by which we speak our experiences to one another. It is not that we cannot record and tell one another of the extraordinary and violent events that have scarred us; it is that these stories conform to a very different set of understandings, conventions, and rules. It is the assumption of this book that the better we understand the underlying rules or grammar of these stories, the better we will grasp the burden of what they have to tell us and the closer we may come to a knowledge that begins exactly where words and "telling" end.

One purpose of this book is to deflate a rhetoric in which these events and their literature is often discussed, a rhetoric that intones but also confuses, an "impossibility" of telling with the functions of such a statement.[1] I am fascinated by the ways that a rhetoric of impossibility plays with and permits a "virtual" trespassing of representational limits. I am interested in the complex ways in which stories of catastrophe take on the epistemological issues extreme experiences raise by so often turning into the story of how the story came to be told, as in Tadeuz Borowski's "World of Stone," Dan Pagis's "The Tower," Aharon Appelfeld's *Badenheim 1939*, or, as we shall see in this very chapter, in Joseph Conrad's *Heart of Darkness*. In each of these cases, the story told is not that of the particular catastrophe but of the telling of (or failure to tell) its story.

In this chapter, I will be concerned with making an important distinction between narratives of "horror" and narratives of "historical horror."[2] The point of my comparison of Edgar Allan Poe's stories "Metzengerstein" and "The Assignation" with Joseph Conrad's *Heart of Darkness* is that the comparison requires us to examine more carefully the specific problematic involved in representing historical horror: in representing events that insist that they cannot be put into words even as they insist upon the need for transmission. These are writings that must invent the means to circumvent their key characteristic—the disbelief that they produce.

When we think of horror in literature, we think of the grotesque, the macabre, the gothic; we think of conventions and strategies of a horror that derives from the imagination. These conventions and strategies are to be found not only in what we have labeled as "gothic," but in all sorts of works, from *Oedipus Rex*, to *King Lear*, to *Crime and Punishment*, in which the projection of horror is an important element of the aesthetic whole. If the classic example of the horror tale is the writing of Edgar Allan Poe, the connection of "horror" to dream and to the imagination is apparent. Richard Wilbur writes that Poe's narrative:

is an allegory of the mind's voyage from the waking world into the world of dreams, with each main step . . . symbolizing the passage of the mind from one to another—from wakefulness to reverie, from reverie to the hypnagogic state, from the hypnagogic state to the deep dream.[3]

Like the tales of Edgar Allan Poe, Joseph Conrad's *Heart of Darkness* is also a symbolic voyage into the horror and evil in the human soul. Conrad, like Poe, relies heavily upon the manipulation of point of view and upon the impressionistic posturings of a central narrative sensibility. And yet his is a very different rendering of horror.

As a literary realization of "horror," Joseph Conrad's *Heart of Darkness* is about a horror that is both more familiar and also, perhaps for that very reason, less well understood—certainly, in literary terms—than horror as we conventionally think of it. It is well known that Conrad's story is based on his own trip to the Congo in 1890; Conrad, in his "Author's Note" to the book edition of his story, famously described *Heart of Darkness* as "experience pushed a little beyond the actual facts of the case. . . ."[4] In *Conrad in the Nineteenth Century*, Ian Watt shows how the novella is part of the polemic of its day, having been written at a moment in which King Leopold and his imperialist policies on the African subcontinent had aroused a storm of criticism.[5] Watt is meticulous in his study of the discrepancies and correspondences of Conrad's text with its biographical and historical background.[6] Similarly, Adam Hochschild, whose recent book, *King Leopold's Ghost*, provides the most detailed account of this period yet to appear, compares Conrad's navigation records and diaries with identical detail appearing in *Heart of Darkness*. Hochschild, who sees Leopold's exploits in the Congo as the beginning of a murderous century of wide-scale opportunistic and genocidal violence, notes the variety of critical spins that *Heart of Darkness* has accumulated since its publication and suggests that:

European and American readers, not comfortable acknowledging the genocidal scale of the killing in

Africa at the turn of the century, have cast 'Heart of Darkness' loose from its historical moorings. We read it as a parable for all times and places, not as a book about one time and place.[7]

As much as Conrad includes an exotic African setting, structures his narrative around a symbolic quest and is fascinated with themes of depravity and madness, the horror he would present is fundamentally different from the invented and aesthetically dictated horror we find in Greek drama, in Shakespeare, or in Poe. In the pages that follow, I will examine the different strategies and assumptions functioning in works by Poe and by Conrad, the one that elaborates deep intuitions of horror from within the human mind, and the other that represents the unmasking and penetration of horror as it exists outside the human mind, in history.

Edgar Allan Poe and the Horror of Fantasy

Asked to adapt Dostoevsky's *The Idiot* for the stage, Milan Kundera wrote that:

> even if I were starving, I could not do the job. Dostoevsky's universe of overblown gestures, murky depths and aggressive sentimentality repelled me. . . . What irritated me about Dostoevsky was the climate of his novels: a universe where everything turns into feeling; in other words, feelings are promoted to the rank and value of truth.[8]

The Dostoevskian world is a world that, for all of its vast embrace and historical reference to place and events, is utterly circumscribed by the feeling-world of its protagonist.[9] The world of Poe, like that of Dostoevsky, is a world in which plot, description, and style point to the internal world of the speaker, only more so. If Dostoevsky works his rich palette on a large canvas, Poe wields his more concentrated effects in precise brush strokes of black and white. And always, story and its elements serve subjective ends. An early Poe story, "Metzengerstein," opens on a note of foreboding: "Horror and fatality have been stalking abroad in all ages."[10] The story details the relationship of the protagonist, a reclusive prince, and a horse that has mysteriously appeared on his property. The mysterious horse is identical to a horse pictured on a family tapestry that the Prince has been studying and it terrifies him. After the real horse appears on the estate, this section of the tapestry is discovered to be missing. Poe notes that no one except the Prince has ever touched the horse.

In other words, the horse is at once real and also supernatural, fabulous, unreal. The mysterious horse both repels and attracts the Prince and eventually races with him into a conflagration that has mysteriously overtaken the palace. The description of the Prince is a study of extremes:

> The agony of his countenance, the convulsive struggle of his frame, gave evidence of superhuman exertion; but no sound, save a solitary shriek, escaped from his lacerated lips, which were bitten through and through in the intensity of terror. . . . (68)

As horse and rider disappear, images of chaos and strife in nature give way to their opposite, to quiet. With the triumph of the horse in the form of a smoke apparition, the inversion of unreal over real is completed:

> The fury of the tempest immediately died away, and a dead calm succeeded. A white flame still enveloped the building like a shroud, and streaming far away into the quiet atmosphere, shot forth a glare of preternatural light; while a cloud of smoke settled heavily over the battlements in the distinct colossal figure of—*a horse*. (69)

The overblown rhetoric of this and other passages and the piling up of typical gothic props and conventions in rapid and melodramatic succession provide the bits and pieces of an anti-realist mode. They form an inverted world of romance and pure invention upon which "historical reality" barely impinges.[11] Within such a mode, character is one-dimensional; history is appropriated as myth as, for example, in "The Pit and the Pendulum" (in which Inquisitorial Spain is another gothic prop), as in Mathew Lewis's *The Monk* (1796), and in a host of other works of gothic imaginings. In all of these works, as in Poe, pitch of emotion ranges from one extreme to another and is more important than variety and kinds of emotion.

It is of interest to observe that while Poe's stories thematize the irrational and ways it can overwhelm the personality, they are not concerned with individual character and psychology. "Metzengerstein" is not about a particular villain, but about fiendishness. Poe's stories are about mythic forces that make destiny inevitable rather than about the intricacies of individual psychology that shape the history and possibilities of the individual. Gothic conventions have no connection to our sense of the historical world in which we live, and function instead as formulas ready at hand to elicit a response of horror from the reader. They are a most unambiguous example of T. S. Eliot's "objective correlative": ". . . a set of objects, a situation, a chain of events which shall be the formula of that particular emotion."[12]

Poe's description in "The Philosophy of Composition" of the writing of his poem, "The Raven," gives insight into his choices, priorities, and concerns as a working artist.[13] In the passage that follows, he treats the question of an appropriate setting in which to place the dialogue of the lovelorn student and the Raven:

> The next point to be considered was the mode of bringing together the lover and the Raven—and the first branch of this consideration was the *locale*. For this the most natural suggestion might seem to be a forest, or the fields—but it has always appeared to me that a close *circumscription of space* is absolutely necessary to the effect of an insulated incident:—it has the force of a frame to a picture. It has an indisputable moral power in keeping concentrated the attention, and, of course, must not be confounded with mere unity of place.

Poe rejects the suggestive possibilities of a natural and open setting for the greater effect upon the reader created by the closed
space of the student's study, "a chamber rendered sacred to him
by memories of her who had frequented it" (460).

This focus upon effect is the counterpart of an anti-realist
mode and is apparent in Poe's use of description in virtually all
of his prose tales. At every moment in a narrative, Poe's aim is
to work the sensibilities of his reader to their utmost. If in so
doing, he can show us something about the workings of the
mind, as in "The Tell Tale Heart," or of the irrational that undermines and overwhelms the mind, as in "Metzengerstein" and
"The Black Cat," so much the better. And the objects, persons,
and events he describes are portrayed not for any value or any
interest they might possess of themselves, but for their value in
producing particular effects upon the reader, including, at certain moments, the revelation of a state of mind.

Here is the narrator's description, in "The Assignation," of
the protagonist of this story:

> There are some subjects upon which I take pleasure in
> being minute. The person of the stranger—let me call
> him by this title, who to all the world was still a
> stranger—the person of the stranger is one of these sub-
> jects. In height he might have been below rather than
> above the medium size: although there were moments of
> intense passion when his frame actually *expanded* and
> belied the assertion.   (73)

Even in these few sentences, which announce themselves as
an excursus in description, there is precious little information—
descriptive or otherwise—provided. In a passage pretending to
describe the proportions of this individual, we find an attempt
at specificity (". . . he might have been below rather than above
medium size: although . . ."), which is a cover for acute linguistic nonsense. The "description" is long. We are told that, under
certain conditions the protagonist's strength is Herculean and
that his mouth and chin are those of a deity. Details accrue that
give no information whatsoever about what they purport to

describe ("Yet his countenance was, nevertheless, one of those which all men have seen at some period of their lives, and have never afterwards seen again.") and which together create a web of association. When, for example, the narrator tells us he has never seen anyone with features as regular, "except, perhaps the marble ones of the Emperor Commodus," associations of marble, statue, kingly rank, and of an ancient Roman past build upon one another in ways that bear no mimetic relationship to life and character, but that draw upon a storehouse of image and reference that is literary, pictorial, and, often, period associated.

Where the utterance, then, is of horror of an imagined origin, a text such as Poe's can afford to indulge and even to luxuriate in the horrors it produces. Poe explains the burden of this strategy in "The Raven":

> The student . . . is impelled, as I have before explained, by the human thirst for self-torture, and in part by superstition, to pro-pound such queries to the bird as will bring him, the lover, the most of the luxury of sorrow, through the anticipated answer "Never-more."

And Poe continues:

> with the indulgence, to the extreme, of this self-torture, the narration . . . has a natural termination. . . .   (462)

Thus, on the one hand, we see in Poe an absolutely ascetic sense of purpose that he brings to his writing, which is such that all elements are subordinated to the creation of effects while, on the other hand, we find an indulgence in the grotesquerie and embellishments of horror that is characteristic of the mode in which he writes.

If Poe's stories fall on one end of a spectrum of literary horror, Conrad's *Heart of Darkness* falls on the other end of the spectrum, where horror originates not from within the mind but from without. As much as Conrad shares with Poe a penchant for melodramatic gesture, for overheated language, an overall commitment to the subjective point of view, and a deep fascination with the human mind, his strategies for the representation of literary horror are the very antithesis of Poe's. A work of horror that draws upon the mind as its source and only point of reference must use every device available to project the horror that is its expressive goal. In such writing, the decibel level of emotion is high while, on the other hand, horror is safely tucked away in the formulas and conventions of an anti-realistic mode. Conversely, where horror is impressed upon the mind by events experienced in the historical world, the writer will seek not to reproduce that horror, but to represent the attempt of the mind to resist and master the horror experienced. This involves the very opposite strategies from those of Poe: strategies of silence, omission, obliqueness, and reticence which present horror in indirect ways, along with a set of strategies that seek to anchor the factuality of a horror whose first characteristic is that it can neither be believed nor put into words.

Joseph Conrad and the Problematic of Historical Horror

At the center of the experience of historical horror is a disbelief that both undermines and shapes the attempt to represent or portray it. Like Poe, Conrad is concerned with the real and the unreal. But the unreal that is so crucial to Marlow's quest in Conrad's *Heart of Darkness* is the unreal, not of fantasy, but of historical events too horrific for description. Hannah Arendt, in *The Origins of Totalitarianism*, describes *Heart of Darkness* as "the most illuminating work on actual race experience in Africa."[14] Conrad captures the stirrings of hope and of greed that fed the Belgian king, Leopold, and the entire imperialist enterprise. Thus, Marlow recounts his visit to the Company offices upon receiving his command: "I had no difficulty in finding the Company offices. It was the biggest thing in town, and everybody I met was full of it. They were going to run an overseas empire, and make no end of coin by trade" (10). Conrad's analysis of the phenomenon of imperialism extends to such unassuming passages as the one in which Marlow meets the Director of the Company:

"A door opened, a white-haired secretarial head, but wearing a compassionate expression, appeared, and a skinny forefinger beckoned me into the sanctuary. Its light was dim, and a heavy writing-desk squatted in the middle. From behind that structure came out an impression of pale plumpness in a frock-coat. The great man himself. He was five feet six, I should judge, and had his grip on the handle-end of ever so many millions. He shook hands, I fancy, murmured vaguely, was satisfied with my French. Bon voyage.   (10)

Marlow, who is usually loquacious and detailed in describing the impressions the surrounding world makes on him, here notes only the height of the Director. The meeting is dramatically abbreviated, foreshortened and condensed. It is not the secretary who appears to usher Marlow into the presence of the "great man," but a "white-haired secretarial head." A "skinny forefinger" signals him to enter the room. Marlow notes such things as the dim light and the desk in the room, without noting in his more usual manner the impression these details make on him.

Of course, this is the very point: the foreshortened description conveys an inhuman quality. Here is no meeting of persons, but of persons dismembered and turned into things. Marlow, like the secretary, his head, and his forefinger, is but an instrument, a cog in the wheel of bureaucracy. This description, as much as any of the more famous passages indicting imperialism, is a dramatic representation of the mode of being and of interacting in the world that made possible, in Conrad's analysis, the devastation and rape of the Congo. Conrad's language, unlike that of Poe, is about the mind interacting with a real historical world out there. However much *Heart of Darkness*, with its exotic setting, its quest structure and other motifs reflects the romantic palette of the period, Conrad writes in a fundamentally realist mode in his preoccupation with and engagement in a real historical world.

Conrad shows us the effects of policies that, according to Hannah Arendt, reduced the peaceful Congo population from between twenty million and forty million in 1890, to eight million in 1911, and which Adam Hochschild more recently described as having created "one of the major killing grounds of modern times."[15] Conrad portrays the black man's thralldom to the white man: "He ought to have been clapping his hands and stamping his feet on the bank, instead of which he was hard at work, a thrall to strange witchcraft, full of improving knowledge" (37). He describes how "strings of dusty niggers with splay feet arrived and departed," and how "a stream of manufactured goods, rubishy cottons, beads, and brass were set into the depths of darkness, and in return came a precious trickle of ivory" (19). He portrays early on and in detail the treatment of the black man:

> "A slight clinking behind me made me turn my head. Six black men advanced in a file, toiling up the path. . . . Black rags were wound round their loins, and the short ends behind wagged to and fro like tails. I could see every rib . . . each had an iron collar on his neck and all were connected together with a chain whose bights swung between them, rhythmically clinking. . . .   (16)

But Conrad's interest in the real world in *Heart of Darkness* goes beyond historical portraiture, beyond description and moral critique of European imperial, commercial, and colonial activities in the Congo. *Heart of Darkness* grapples with an opacity at the heart of historical catastrophe that robs us of our ability to meaningfully come to terms with the most disastrous events of human history.

Two Narratives of Knowing

Catastrophe, by its nature, exceeds the ability of the mind to grasp it. Its facts are, at one and the same time, known and not known; they blind, confuse, and enlighten all at once. They call out for narrative and insist that they are part of a narrative at the same time that they refuse to be contained within narrative. In

Heart of Darkness Conrad is concerned with the epistemological, psychological, and narrative issues that are the defining marks of catastrophic historical experience. He is concerned with what Cathy Caruth calls the "unclaimed experience" of historical trauma, with the contested status within consciousness, of catastrophic or traumatic fact.[16]

Or, better, he is concerned with fact and traumatic fact, and with the distinct paths of apprehension that each calls upon. At one point Marlow marvels that the starving cannibals on his steamship do not eat him and his passengers:

> "Don't you know the devilry of lingering starvation, its exasperating torment, its black thought, its somber and brooding ferocity? Well, I do. It takes a man all his inborn strength to fight hunger properly. It's really easier to face bereavement, dishonour, and the perdition of one's soul—than this kind of prolonged hunger. Sad but true. And these chaps had no earthly reason for any kind of scruple. Restraint! I would just as soon have expected restraint from a hyena prowling amongst the corpses of a battlefield. But there was the fact facing me—the fact dazzling, to be seen, like the foam on the depths of the sea, like a ripple on an unfathomable enigma. . . .   (42, 43)

The "fact" at issue is one of great historical importance since it is this mysterious "restraint" of the black man that helped make possible the repeated degradation and colonization of the black masses in the Congo and across Africa by a relatively small European presence. Conrad lingers on that fact: "the fact facing me—the fact dazzling, to be seen, like the foam on the depths of the sea, like a ripple on an unfathomable enigma."

Conrad is preoccupied, then, in *Heart of Darkness*, with fact, with the idea of fact, with the perceptual and epistemological issues that surround fact. Fact, like the foam that rides atop a cresting wave, or like a ripple that disturbs the surface of a body of water, calls attention to itself and disconcerts our picture of things. It "dazzles." It is experienced in sensory, physical terms like a sliver of light that irritates the eye as it "dazzles." The light blinds but also illuminates. Conrad's language suggests an imaginative path of grappling with fact, a path that moves from initial wonder and apprehension of fact to its physical and bodily integration.

Two more weighted instances occur in which simple objects come to signify a state of ultimate integration and facticity that is morally and symbolically charged. Marlow is much concerned with the rivets which lie uselessly about in crates at other trading posts and which he now needs to fix the tin pot steamship that is to pick up Kurtz. "What I really wanted was rivets, by Heaven! Rivets. To get on with the work—to stop the hole . . ." Marlow exclaims to one of the trading agents (30). A page later he continues: ". . . but what I wanted was a certain quantity of rivets—and rivets were what Mr. Kurtz wanted if he had only known it" (31). The quest for Kurtz and for the knowledge Kurtz possesses cannot get under way without the rivets to hold the steamship together. Rivets are needed quite literally, then, for structural connection and symbolize, by virtue of that function and of their physical properties, an integration of self and world that is the foundation of knowing and the goal of Marlow's quest.

After three months of delay, the voyage to the Inner Station and to Kurtz begins. Along the way, Marlow and the pilgrims come upon an unlikely but "significant" object, a sailor's book left in an abandoned hut in the middle of the jungle. Marlow picks it up:

> "It had lost its covers, and the pages had been thumbed into a state of extremely dirty softness; but the back had been lovingly stitched afresh with white cotton thread, which looked clean yet. It was an extraordinary find. Its title was *An Inquiry into Some Points of Seamanship*, by a man Towser, Towson—some such name—Master in His Majesty's Navy. The matter looked dreary reading enough, with illustrative diagrams and repulsive tables of figures, and the copy was sixty years old. I handled this amazing antiquity with the greatest possible tenderness, lest it should dissolve in my hands. Within, Towson

or Towser was inquiring earnestly into the breaking strain of ships' chains and tackle, and other such matters. Not a very enthralling book; but at the first glance you could see there a singleness of intention, an honest concern for the right way of going to work, which make these humble pages, thought out so many years ago, luminous with another than a professional light. The simple old sailor, with his talk of chains and purchases, made me forget the jungle and the pilgrims in a delicious sensation of having come upon something unmistakably real. (38, 39)

Once again, fact calls forth astonishment and investigation before it yields up its meaning. Marlow ponders the content and purposes of the book; it is "an extraordinary find," a book that is filled with "repulsive tables of figures" but that, upon reflection, is "luminous with another than a professional light." Again, the formulation of meaning is experiential, and, in its literary representation, takes a sensory, nonverbal form. To stumble upon this "delicious sensation of having come upon something unmistakably real," is to move somewhere past the physical object or fact to its integration within a human consciousness. The passage describes knowing as a process, as a journey of consciousness into a world of physical, historical and human fact, and consciousness as something that exists as a primary awareness within the body. The cannibals' restraint, the rivets, and the book are parts of a world of fact outside mind and consciousness, facts that call forth on the part of Marlow a complex journey of consciousness seeking to take in those facts, their meaning, their perceived "reality" or facticity.

The central quest of the novella is really about the problem of fact and how we can know fact, especially where the fact involved is catastrophic. And it is this problematic of catastrophic fact—of fact that is, finally, unknowable—that shapes *Heart of Darkness* as a journey, not toward the object itself since, in any case, that object cannot be known, but toward Kurtz, the European agent who has participated in the horror and gives testimony to that horror in his famous dying words. *Heart of Darkness* is not the story of the white man's shocking behavior in Africa, but the story of Marlow's journey to receive Kurtz's testimony about that shocking behavior.

Conrad's meditation on fact and on questions around the knowing and telling of fact in *Heart of Darkness* suggests that where the subject is historical catastrophe, one path of knowing and telling must be laid aside in favor of a very different way of knowing and telling. It is as though Conrad offers us, in the course of *Heart of Darkness*, two different narratives of knowing. The first, including the stories of the cannibals, the rivets, and the book, is the story of how we may know objects in an essentially familiar and knowable, and therefore also representable, world. This is a narrative in which the objects—the cannibals, the rivets, the book—take center stage, and the process of knowing involves a movement or journey within the consciousness of the individual. Such a journey is temporal in nature and is therefore narratable: it can be put into words, told in the form of a story, shared with others. Narrative itself functions as a means or form of knowing for the reader. The second narrative of knowing, the story of Marlow and his quest—the story of how we may know objects that fall outside the familiar representable world—is a very different narrative. It is also about an object, but one that is consistently experienced and described in *Heart of Darkness* as "unreal," and thereby unknowable. And it is about a process of knowing that relies on the experiences and knowledge of someone else—of a witness. The knowledge gained is thus second-hand, indirect, distinctly social, and also deeply problematic. Marlow journeys upriver to hear Kurtz's testimony, testimony he then betrays and fails to pass on to Kurtz's Intended but that, at the same time, he does indeed transmit in the course of telling his tale to his cronies on board the *Nellie*—including to the narrator, and through the narrator, to the reader.

The narrative of *Heart of Darkness*, then, is double. It includes an untold story—the utter horror of catastrophic experience that cannot be put into words—as well as the story of a journey to hear the story of a witness to that horror. Marlow's journey to hear Kurtz's voice functions as a sort of default narrative that comes into play precisely when and where direct knowing as a narratable act of the individual consciousness is not possible. The narrative of historical horror in *Heart of Darkness* involves us in an omitted, as well as substituted, narrative. The point of the substituted narrative (Marlow's journey to hear Kurtz's story) is exactly that: that it is a substitution, that it leaves intact—morally, aesthetically, structurally, formally—an opacity or silence at the heart of historical catastrophe. The story that cannot be told, *is not told*. It is the integrity of this omitted narrative, and the utter negation that is thereby foregrounded within the larger structure of such a double narrative, that marks a boundary separating what is representable from what is not. This clear and clearly marked boundary brings the unrepresentable, if not into view for the reader, within some sort of existential, or felt, proximity.

Thus, while Conrad provides us, in *Heart of Darkness*, with a narrative of knowing the world in its knowability and representability (the restraint of the cannibals, the rivets, the book), he also provides us with its opposite, with a narrative about the impossibility of knowing (and thereby, also, of representing) where the knowledge at stake involves experiences of historical catastrophe. And he provides us with a modality of knowing—a "witnessed" modality—that comes into play exactly where words and stories fall apart, where events disengage themselves from a sense of the "real," of the plausible, of the remotely possible.

It is where traumatic fact cannot articulate itself credibly in words or story that narrative falls back on a witnessed mode of knowing. Kurtz, like the horror to which he is witness, is mostly absent from *Heart of Darkness* except for his final testimonial words:

> "Anything approaching the change that came over his features I have never seen before and hope never to see again. . . . It was as though a veil had been rent. . . . Did he live his life again in every detail of desire, temptation, and surrender during that supreme moment of complete

knowledge? He cried in a whisper at some image, at some vision—he cried out twice, a cry that was no more than a breath:

"'The horror! The horror!' (70, 71)

A veil is rent, a revelation takes place at this climactic moment of "complete knowledge," but the content of this knowledge is never fully articulated. Unlike the journey of consciousness undertaken in order to apprehend fully and completely the fact of the cannibals' restraint or the "meaning" of the rivets and of the book, this knowledge seems to involve the opposite: a meaning or effect that is detached from its referent. If a veil is rent, only Kurtz can see behind this veil and give testimony to what he sees. Marlow merely responds to Kurtz's facial expressions and listens to his voice, to his "cry that was no more than a breath." He is privy to a truth at which he did not arrive through an act of his consciousness, but one that he receives and passes on to others. He is witness to the witness in a narrative mode that centers on a relay of witnesses and that comes into play exactly when, and because, other forms of knowing are not available.[17]

Narrating Unrepresentability

Marlow's voyage, a voyage to "make real" the unreal, involves the turning from a narrative to a witnessed form of knowing, the elements of which include an untold or omitted narrative and its substitute narrative—the journey to hear the story of the witness. The narration of unrepresentability does not move from fact to meaning to the integration of meaning as with the cannibals, the rivets, and the book; it moves from the unreality of certain facts, to the sensed "reality" and truth of other facts, to the testimony provided by Kurtz, and its problematic transmission.

Thus, the European presence in Africa, the horror and exploitation made possible by the bureaucratic system, the treatment of the black man, and the description of life at the trading stations occur for the most part in the first section of *Heart of*

Darkness as we follow Marlow from Europe to the shores of Africa and to the Central Station where he finds the vessel he is to command at the bottom of the river. These are the unintegrated facts of historical existence that Conrad lays before us, facts that Conrad consistently describes as "unreal" by contrast to the African natives, the jungle, the sea, the rivets, and the book, which are described as conveying a sense of "the real" to Marlow. In the passage that follows, Conrad describes Marlow's first view of Africa from on board a passenger ship carrying him to the first of several trading stations. Already the historical, physical, and sensory "facts" of the world around him are categorized into those that seem to be a delusion and those that are natural, that have reason and meaning; those that keep Marlow away from the truth of things and those that "gave one a momentary contact with reality":

"We pounded along, stopped, landed soldiers; went on, landed custom-house clerks to levy toll in what looked like a god-forsaken wilderness, with a tin shed and a flag-pole lost in it: landed more soldiers—to take care of the custom-house clerks presumably. Some, I heard, got drowned in the surf; but whether they did or not, nobody seemed particularly to care. They were just flung out there, and on we went. . . . The idleness of a passenger, my isolation amongst all these men with whom I had no point of contact, the oily and languid sea, the uniform sombreness of the coast, seemed to keep me away from the truth of things, within the toil of a mournful and senseless delusion. The voice of the surf heard now and then was a positive pleasure, like the speech of a brother. It was something natural, that had its reason, that had a meaning. Now and then a boat from the shore gave one a momentary contact with reality. It was paddled by black fellows. You could see from afar the white of their eyeballs glistening. They shouted, sang; their bodies streamed with perspiration; they had faces like grotesque masks—these chaps; but they had bone, muscle, a wild vitality, an intense energy of movement, that was as natural and true as the surf along their coast. They wanted no excuse for being there. They were a great comfort to look at. For a time I would feel I belonged still to a world of straightforward facts; but the feeling would not last long. . . . (13, 14)

As in the descriptions of the rivets and of the book, the material and the sensuous are explicitly linked to "truth" and experienced as factual and real. The black men paddling their boats along the shore are "a great comfort" for Marlow "to look at," and he describes the black men themselves in triumphantly sensuous terms: "but they had bone, muscle, a wild vitality, an intense energy of movement, that was as natural and true as the surf along their coast."

Throughout *Heart of Darkness*, then, the unchanging, exotic, and fabulous jungle and its people are associated, in Conrad's words, with vitality, energy, nature, truth, meaning, straightforward fact, purpose, and reality while the traders and the European world they represent are just as consistently described as (the adjectives in both cases are Conrad's) dissembling, cruel, inhuman, sham, hollow, rapacious, ludicrous, muddled, flabby, greedy, without seriousness, and absurd. Significantly, Marlow feels isolated among the traders whom he calls—here and elsewhere—"phantoms," so that he is positioned throughout *Heart of Darkness* between the two, between the unreality of the world of the traders and the reality and truth of the world of the jungle:

> "They wandered here and there with their absurd long staves in their hands, like a lot of faithless pilgrims bewitched inside a rotten fence. . . . By Jove! I've never seen anything so unreal in my life. And outside, the silent wilderness surrounding this cleared speck on the earth struck me as something great and invincible like evil or truth, waiting patiently for the passing of this fantastic invasion. (23)

Thus the world around Marlow is one that is fragmented into pieces that Marlow experiences as real, and pieces that Marlow

experiences as unreal. As Marlow journeys upriver toward
Kurtz, the jungle becomes a more active presence and organizing motif, taking over from the shabby and destructive world of
the trading stations. His journey progresses from a world of the
unreal (historical, traders) to the world of the real (natives, jungle), a journey that is indeed about a fragmentation within the
experiencing subject that persists and that cannot achieve integration except through the agency of another (Kurtz), and even
then only temporarily.

Historical Horror and the Strategies of Silence

The portrait of unrepresentability, then, involves the silence
of a story that cannot be told along with another story, the story
of Marlow's witnessing. Where the object of knowledge is horrific, the object remains silent and speaks, at best, only through
the testimony of others.

Horror, because it is the word that Kurtz uses to sum up his
judgment of himself, bears the accumulated weight of all that
draws Marlow onward to meet Kurtz. It is the revelation
promised, deferred, sought, and revealed. Narrative time slows
as we draw closer and closer to Kurtz and the meanings
promised, not because Conrad indulges in leisured description
of a primeval landscape, its sounds, its imposing reality, but
because the sounds and silences and stillness are part of an
inner resistance, part of that which shrinks before a fully experienced illumination of "'The horror! The horror!'"

Horror is the most significant word in this work, and it is
also the most sparingly used "significant" word. Except for
Kurtz's cry, it appears four or five times in a narrative of close to
eighty pages. It appears for the first time in Marlow's description of the "gloomy circle of some Inferno" to which the sick and
diseased blacks retreat to die (17). Marlow describes himself as
"horrorstruck" at the sight which is like "some picture of a massacre or a pestilence" (18).

This reticence with respect to the word "horror" takes other
forms as well. Marlow reacts to the sight of human suffering in

this and in every instance by turning away where possible: "I didn't want any more loitering in the shade, and I made haste towards the station," he says, just as earlier he tries to let a chained gang of blacks he has described in some detail get out of sight: "You know I am not particularly tender . . . ," he avers and stands "appalled, as though by a warning" (17, 18).

Marlow talks a great deal and yet says little about himself. At one point he describes his puttering to get the tinpot steamship going and ends the paragraph, "I toiled wearily in a wretched scrapheap unless I had the shakes too bad to stand" (70). This is the first hint of an illness we never hear about except one more time when Marlow tells us: "And it is not my own extremity I remember best. . . . No! It is his extremity that I seem to have lived through" (72). Just as he glosses over his own brush with death, he glosses over the hardships of a two hundred mile trek for fifteen days by foot through jungle to the Central Station, during which such mishaps occur as the disappearance of all of the black carriers who dump Marlow's overweight and sick, white companion in the bush: "However all that is to no purpose," Marlow comments (21).

All of these incidents and passages point to horror while, at the same time, they maintain a reticence. At odd moments Marlow mentions that he has not eaten and is getting savage or that a new pair of shoes he just threw overboard is splattered with the blood of his black helmsman. In each case Marlow continues his meditative and essentially detached narration; we hear about the stillness of the jungle or the impact of Kurtz's words on him as though he had never mentioned his more personal struggle with the brutalizing conditions of his journey and their effects upon him. Marlow is constantly trying to point out the significance of things; he recounts the impressions that people, events, and environment make on him. He observes. He characterizes, judges what he sees. But he leaves out the gut line, the experience going on inside Marlow out of which his speech flows.

Conrad litters his text with examples of physical brutality and of casual death, all of which are parenthetic: glimpsed and quickly passed over. Marlow's command is the result of a strange incident in which the former captain, Fresleven, "the gentlest, quietest creature that ever walked on two legs," quarrels over some hens and publicly and mercilessly beats a screaming black chieftain whose desperate son then spears and kills the gentle Danish captain. Marlow refrains from describing Fresleven's death and observes instead that the black man's spear "of course . . . went quite easy between the shoulder-blades" (9). Later, he describes a delivery of letters to a French ship absurdly firing shells into the "empty immensity of earth, sky, and water": "We gave her letters (I heard the men in that lonely ship were dying of fever at the rate of three a day) and went on" (14).

The use of parentheses here is deliberate. On his two hundred mile foot journey through the wilderness, Marlow passes several black carriers "dead in harness, at rest in the long grass near the path" (20). Significantly, Conrad follows this example of casual death with a description of the silence of the jungle, a powerful, felt silence that seems to absorb into itself all of the inarticulate outrage that casual death inflicts upon the living and that we sense in the sound of drumming that follows the silence:

> "Now and then a carrier dead in harness, at rest in the long grass near the path, with an empty water-gourd and his long staff lying by his side. A great silence around and above. Perhaps on some quiet night the tremor of far-off drums, sinking, swelling, a tremor vast, faint; a sound weird, appealing, suggestive, and wild— and perhaps with as profound a meaning as the sound of bells in a Christian country. (20)

Like the rest of the "pilgrims," Marlow feels "bewitched and cut off for ever from everything . . . amongst the overwhelming realities of this strange world of plants, water, and silence" (34). The silence of the jungle is here connected to Marlow's feeling of being cut off and disconnected from the world around him. A page later, Marlow describes the sense of being cut off and overwhelmed in the following way:

"We were cut off from the comprehension of our sur-
roundings; we glided past like phantoms, wondering
and secretly appalled, as sane men would be before an
enthusiastic outbreak in a madhouse. We could not
understand because we were too far and could not
remember. . . . (36)

The jungle is both an imagined, integrated, human, and origi-
nary world with which Marlow and the Europeans have lost
contact, and a horrifying projection of the potential for evil
within themselves, which Marlow and the others sense but do
not yet "comprehend."

Marlow, we have seen, is loquacious and, at the same time,
closed. He selectively understates, turns away from the sight of
death and atrocity, speaks in a voice that is essentially imper-
sonal at the same time that it is subjective, and feels cut off and
appalled by what he sees and experiences. Finally, he displaces
and projects all he turns away from onto the jungle "world of
plants, water, and silence." The frequency of Marlow's use of
the word *silence* is as startling as the infrequency of his use of the
word *horror*, and the two are closely related. Marlow is preoccupied with silence, with the "indeterminable miles of silence"
before him "while we crept toward Kurtz" (38), with the "high
stillness of primeval forest" before his eyes (27), with the jungle
as a "rioting invasion of soundless life" (13), with the "audible
soothing silence" that follows the drum beats and cries of the
natives (65). The word is repeated in myriad ways, always
ambiguously and suggestively:

". . . and through the dim stir, through the faint sounds
of that lamentable courtyard, the silence of the land went
home to one's very heart—its mystery, its greatness, the
amazing reality of its concealed life. (26)

The silence and its mystery are indeed the reality, or better,
the horror that Marlow would like to conceal and that he walks
away from at every opportunity. *Heart of Darkness* is carefully
orchestrated not only to reveal, but also to conceal. For all of its

sympathy for the exploited, it is crucial to note that the story is narrated from the perspective of the perpetrator—of a member and employee of those who are exploiting the native population. A sentence such as "Black shapes crouched, lay, . . . clinging to the earth . . . in all the attitudes of pain, abandonment, and despair," would read very differently had it been written from the perspective of one of the dying blacks or from the eyes of the dying man's child, brother, or wife (17). Marlow and Kurtz's horror is not the horror of the victim, tortured and abandoned by his fellow man, but a wrenching form of insight into the human capacity for and complicity with evil. The two perspectives are entirely different, and the second is in some ways more devastating, more complex and problematic, but also less emotional at its core.

Silence, then, in *Heart of Darkness,* takes forms that are explicit as well as implicit, tonal as well as structural. While the evidence of human devastation does appear in Conrad's text, the weight, passion, and focus of the narrative have been displaced: dramatically, onto the symbolic quest-journey, and linguistically, onto images and onto a rhetoric associated with the jungle, its sounds, the cries heard, and, especially, its silence. Silence as an image, in *Heart of Darkness,* acquires a life and density of its own, even as, within the narrative of the quest and again in the lie to the Intended, Conrad acknowledges that other, more awful, silence that cannot be broken.

Overcoming Disbelief: Strategies of Authentication

After permitting one of the trading agents, a brickmaker, to think he has influence with the Company offices in Europe, Marlow reflects:

> "I became in an instant as much of a pretence as the rest of the bewitched pilgrims. This simply because I had a notion it somehow would be of help to that Kurtz whom at the time I did not see—you understand. He was just a word for me. I did not see the man in the name any more

than you do. Do you see him? Do you see anything? It seems to me I am trying to tell you a dream—making a vain attempt, because no relation of a dream can convey the dream-sensation, that commingling of absurdity, surprise, and bewilderment in a tremor of struggling revolt, that notion of being captured by the incredible which is of the very essence of dreams. . . ."   (27, 28)

The question of how to find words to relate the "incredible," to make real the unreal, is the highly self-conscious project of *Heart of Darkness*. Kurtz's gift is the gift of language, and the entire period of the voyage and meeting with Kurtz is portrayed in a series of adjectives that describe the way things sound. "A voice. He was little more than a voice," Marlow says and describes the memory of his stay in Africa in the unlikely image of the sound of "a dying vibration of one immense jabber, silly, atrocious, savage, or simply mean without any kind of sense" (49). Sounds, whether they be the sound of drums or of silence, the "flying terror of the sound" of a steam whistle or the "infinite desolation" of a human cry, repeat through the text in leitmotifs that together project a world of sound and expression that has not yet differentiated into speech, into words and forms that represent.

Indeed, the key event toward which the larger narrative moves is not arrival at a physical location or even a moral destination, but an event of vocalization. It is Kurtz's whisper: "a cry that was no more than a breath" and the reception of that whisper (71). The factuality or integration that is the goal of Marlow's quest-voyage is accomplished by the action of Kurtz's cry and, more specifically, by the communication of lived knowledge from one man to another through the living and bodily medium of the voice, and in the modulations and inflections of that voice.

One of the most interesting aspects of the novella is the fact that it is structured around this very idea of personal communication, of telling and listening: of telling that claims the status of witnessed truth, of listening that establishes a line of transmission in society for that truth.[17] Conrad underlines the personal relationship of witness and listener upon which this sense of the real relies. He describes Marlow's first interchange with Kurtz: "I did say the right thing . . . at this very moment, when the foundations of our intimacy were being laid—to endure—to endure—even to the end—even beyond" (67).

If Marlow's journey is climaxed by an act of listening, the larger work is structured as a series of "tellings." Kurtz's personal revelation of witnessed truth is passed on to Marlow, who tells his story to the five men aboard the *Nellie*. That story is told to the reader by one of Marlow's five listeners, who describes their bonding and the community they constitute:

> Between us there was, as I have already said somewhere, the bond of the sea. Besides holding our hearts together through long periods of separation, it had the effect of making us tolerant of each other's yarns—and even convictions. (3)

Heart of Darkness shapes itself, then, not as the narrative of something that happened but as a story about telling which is conceived as an exchange between a teller and his or her community. This telling is of a special kind, the speech of a witness, Kurtz, relayed through Marlow to a community, and through the narrator—who is of that community that has gathered and is listening to Marlow aboard the *Nellie*—to us.

But Marlow never tells us what he actually sees when he glances into Kurtz's cabin. Instead, he describes his disbelief, his shock, and the outcry he might have made:

> "I think I would have raised an outcry if I had believed my eyes. But I didn't believe them at first—the thing seemed so impossible. The fact is I was completely unnerved by sheer blank fright, pure abstract terror. . . . What made this emotion so overpowering was—how shall I define it?—the moral shock I received, as if something altogether monstrous, intolerable to thought and odious to the soul, had been thrust upon me unexpectedly. (65)

The notion of witnessing and the religious language in which Conrad later describes Kurtz's deathbed revelation confer a status of truth and factuality upon events that, in themselves, are "intolerable to thought and odious to the soul," and so resist belief, resist words, resist representation.

The witnessing modality around which *Heart of Darkness* is structured is a function, then, of an essential unrepresentability that, in turn, makes even the possibility of adequate witnessing problematic. *Heart of Darkness* brings the reader one line of successful witnessing and transmission: Kurtz's testimony is passed on to Marlow, from Marlow to his cronies aboard the *Nellie* including the narrator, and through the narrator to the reader. And it brings the reader a second line of witnessing and transmission, one which falls apart in the face of historical horror that is so extensive that it resists witnessing, and cannot establish a line of transmission for events that will thus remain veiled from society by resistance and denial. I am referring here to Marlow's famous lie to Kurtz's Intended. The transmission of witnessed "truth" is successful in the one instance and unsuccessful in the other, so that *Heart of Darkness* explores the impossibility of knowing, within which even a knowing that sidesteps the issue of representation by adopting a modality of witness remains fundamentally problematic and elusive.

Marlow's encounter with Kurtz in Africa is thus followed by his encounter with Kurtz's Intended in Europe from whom Marlow conceals Kurtz's final words: "I could not tell her. It would have been too dark—too dark altogether. . . ." The effect of Marlow's lie to the Intended is to suggest that the human truths Marlow has wrested from the heart of imperialist and historical darkness are finally useless, demoralizing, and even dangerous for the conduct and support of life in the real world. The same narrative that is structured upon a relay of witnesses presents us with the dilemma of the witness who fears the consequences of his witnessing. *Heart of Darkness* brings us the story of Marlow's witnessing as well as the story of Marlow's decision to bear false witness.

If the real is constituted in society by an act of witnessing, the lie to the Intended brings to naught the animating quest of the novella, or at least, turns it on its head. The lived truth of the witness defers, finally, to the necessary fictions of survival. The unbearable knowledge is suppressed in the human arena while, in the form of art, Conrad exposes the modalities, resistances, and difficulties of that knowing. So accurate is Conrad in his imaginative and analytic grasp of the behaviors and situation he dramatizes, that the story resonates almost a century later with the authority of prophecy: Western civilization has indeed deceived itself for the hundred years following the writing of Conrad's novella, into unprecedented programs of enslavement, of ethnic and racial cleansings, and of state-sanctioned extermination.

Chapter 2

The Silence of Historical Traumatic Experience:
Aharon Appelfeld's *Badenheim 1939*

> Mystery on the border of death
> Lay a finger upon your lips:
> 'Silence Silence Silence'-
> —*Nelly Sachs*

The previous chapter examined an essential unrepresentability or silence in Conrad's *Heart of Darkness*. The point of Marlow's voyage to hear Kurtz's famous whisper is that the whisper is Kurtz's testimony to a narrative that is never told. Even this testimony is finally betrayed, sealing the silence of an unrepresentability that figures in all narratives of historical horror. We meet this narrative omission or silence again and again in works of historical horror: a pointing to a story that remains untold, usually accompanied by a substitute narrative, perhaps about the effort to tell the untold story, or, as in *Heart of Darkness*, about receiving the story from the mouth of a witness. Such a double structure is indeed the case of Aharon Appelfeld's small Hebrew masterpiece, *Badenheim 1939* (translated into English and first published in 1980), which is the subject of this chapter.[1]

33

To understand some of the aesthetic ramifications of a text of historical horror, it helps to refer to the visual arts and think of narratives of historical horror as reversing the usual relationship of positive and negative compositional space. What is really foregrounded in works of historical horror is the blank of a negative or empty space (all that Kurtz refers to but omits when he whispers, "The horror! The horror!"), and what is backgrounded is the positive or filled space (the literal narrative of Marlow's quest to find Kurtz), space that always points away from itself to the foregrounded narrative silence that is the mark of traumatic historical experience.[2]

This foregrounded silence involves a very specific kind of unrepresentability, one that is linked to traumatic historical experience. It consists of that *within catastrophic experience* that exceeds and lies outside words—a silence so dense with historical process, death, contingency, and chaos, that the mere glimpse of it (Kurtz's famous whisper of horror, for example) threatens to eclipse the order inevitably implied by the literal narrative of Marlow's journey to find Kurtz. In this sense, Marlow's lie to the Intended restores a balance that is shattered by the glimpse Kurtz provides into the unrepresentable heart of historical trauma. Thus the literal "background" narrative bears within it a certain fragility; it is always marked by the knowledge that it cannot perform its appointed task, the existential task of all words, narrative, literature and art: to reduce the death, loss, and contingency of historical existence to manageable proportions.

Badenheim 1939 includes a double narrative, the narrative of an extermination that remains untold and outside the borders of the novella (the foregrounded silence), and a narrative that alludes to the struggle around expression and its impossibility in the story of the fortunes and misfortunes of the summer music festival at Badenheim (the substitute narrative). What follows is a study of how the traumatic silence proceeding from the experience of "historical horror" structures a work of art, and how a particular work of art orchestrates and represents this silence that falls outside the words, forms, and conventions of representation.

Omission: Silence as Structure

Badenheim 1939 imagines a place in Europe called Baden-heim—a counterpart, perhaps, to Marienbad, a spa in western Czechoslovakia famous for its mineral springs and baths. Badenheim is a summer resort typical of so many other European spas to which an assortment of guests flock each summer to nurse body and soul with a fare of concerts, good food, long walks through the town and adjoining forests, poetry readings, and agreeable company. But the year is not imagined. It is historically specific and that specificity is crucial to the novel.

It is spring, 1939. The hotel is readying itself for the guests who will descend upon the sleepy and slow-moving town. And we are also told, somewhat vaguely, that "It had been a strange, hard winter. Storms had swept through the town and torn the roofs off the houses. Rumors were rife" (7).

The strangeness ascribed to the winter and the word *rumor* point in the direction of a historical specificity which has entered the story and yet is kept at a certain distance within it. It is, after all, nine months after the occupation of the Sudetenland in which Badenheim is presumably located, a bit over two months before the German invasion of Poland on September 1, which launches World War II. If Appelfeld leaves us, historically, at the very brink of war, he ends his story, similarly, at the brink of an extermination that takes place outside the frame of the novel. The extermination of the Jews of Badenheim is anticipated virtually from the first paragraph of the novel, in which inspectors from the Sanitation Department, the administrative arm of government responsible for the effort to cleanse the world of its Jews, already make their appearance. Events, relationships, and conversation in *Badenheim 1939* are conditioned by an understanding among the characters of what lies ahead and by an unspoken agreement among the characters to seek out ways to deny what they cannot afford to recognize and what Appelfeld has so carefully relegated just beyond the circle of his story.

As the novel closes, the Jews of Badenheim gather at the train station. A freight train appears. The scene is not unfamiliar. The reader knows exactly what the freight car portends. The fate anticipated in the opening paragraph of the novel, is at hand—or almost. The novel closes on a note not of recognition but of denial, not with the extermination but with the instant just prior to it:

> An engine, an engine coupled to four filthy freight cars, emerged from the hills and stopped at the station. Its appearance was as sudden as if it had risen from a pit in the ground. "Get in!" yelled invisible voices. And the people were sucked in. Even those who were standing with a bottle of lemonade in their hands, a bar of chocolate, the headwaiter with his dog—they were all sucked in as easily as grains of wheat poured into a funnel. Nevertheless, Dr. Pappenheim found time to make the following remark: "If the coaches are so dirty it must mean that we have not far to go."   (175)

Pappenheim's final words give voice to the impossibility of the mind to assimilate the horror of genocide in such immediate terms as the four filthy train cars into which the Jews of Badenheim (and, metaphorically, the rest of European Jewry) are "sucked in as easily as grains of wheat poured into a funnel." Collapsed into a single moment that occurs just immediately outside the "fiction," the genocide of Badenheim's Jews gains the force of a body in motion suddenly stopped short. Its impact draws precisely on the long preparation, the continuous motion toward, and stopping short before an envisioned destination: the awful, unmentionable, and literally unwritable event.

The novel plays endlessly with an imagery of sound and of silence against the backdrop of this larger silence. The night before the Jews of Badenheim are to meet the trains and their fate, some of the characters get together to "celebrate" the fortieth birthday of one of the group, Gertie. Gertie herself informs the company that "'The emigration procedures have been posted on the notice boards'" (148). The party, understandably, lacks gaiety. People lack words to speak. They sink in their armchairs as though they are about to disappear forever into them while, contrastingly:

The colored wall, adorned with reproductions seemed to come alive: it was as if dormant veins had started to throb in it. Nocturnal shadows slunk against the windows and a fat fly beat against the screens. If there were any words left, they belonged to Salo. But Salo did not speak. . . .

We feel a hush as the lights dim and life energies on the verge of extinction drain into rooms that have, until now, contained those lives:

> The lights grew dimmer, and delicate sounds invaded the room from outside. It seemed that the country parlor was already living a life of its own, a life without people.
>
> (150)

A kind of transubstantiation has occurred here, an exchange of vitality between the inanimate world and those who have always inhabited it. The loss of vitality includes a loss of speech: "Salo did not speak. . . ." But the silence is itself never specified. Instead Appelfeld writes ". . . and delicate sounds invaded the room from outside." The silence here is neither named nor described but appears in a negative form, in the form of an absence. The sounds and words that normally fill human spaces are located somewhere "outside" the room being described, a room whose silence is literally wordless and is perceptible only by virtue of those sounds that "invaded the room from outside."

In an early discussion of traumatic syndrome, Robert Lifton writes that "In order to dissociate itself from grotesque death, the mind must itself cease to live, become itself deadened."[3] There is an intimate connection in the passage between the loss of vitality and a loss of speech that afflicts the guests at Gertie's party. The characters die into a silence that is death-like and that, in some unnerving and prescient manner, speaks the obliteration that lies ahead, and before which they have numbed themselves. The party scene tracks the process of this psychic dying, which ends in a silence that does not so much suffuse or fill the space in which it is enclosed, as it consists of an ebbing and draining away of all life traces, and, foremost, of words.

Badenheim 1939 is a novel with a double frame, one that is literal, begins with the beginning of the novel and ends with the end of the novel and the other that stretches beyond it to include all that is excluded and denied. The point of this other, "implied" frame, is exactly that: that it is an implied, not an explicit structure. The drama of the novel derives from the necessity of implying what cannot be stated, and in this oblique but powerful way opening up, indeed foregrounding, the silence of a fate for which there are no words.

The juxtaposition of frames privileges the world of silence, a world of meanings that insist and press their unanswerable questionings upon us. We read, as it were, in a different space, in a special zone of hearing. And that altered balance between a world of silence and a world of words is reflected in the flow of terse, symbolic narrative, of charged poetic association, of images that are ambiguous, or, like Dr. Pappenheim's own final words, evasive, deliberately unexplained, and hence, always pointing toward some other explanation, toward some organizing logos that refuses to be named. It imbues the reality at hand with the sense of something akimbo, jagged, disconnected, and yet, in some other, deeper and terrifying way, connected.

When the schoolgirl lover of one of the older men suddenly stands up and asks, "Why don't you take me out of here? Can't you see that I can't stand it any longer?" her outburst is unexpected. And her question is left hanging in the air, unanswered. The effect is surreal. We sense a reality and meaning that are just beyond our grasp, an ultimacy beyond the narrative that drains the ordinary of its vitality, its sacred center, its organization. And it is frightening. There is a sense of panic. The girl faints. Someone orders brandy. There is a poise, a balance that breaks down far too easily and too quickly:

> Thus the twilight hour was shattered. Shutz knelt down and lifted her onto the sofa. The people stood around her looking chastised, as if the facts of life had suddenly given them a slap in the face.   (77)

Another passage, again concerning the pregnant schoolgirl, begins by peeling away the reality of words to close on a similar strange note of harshness and disappointment:

> Darkness fell and the words died away. The schoolgirl's face grew more and more transparent. There was no fear or regret in her eyes. It was as if she weren't a girl who had run away from school, but a young woman who had known both pleasure and disappointments in her life: she curled up in the blankets like an experienced woman who knew the value of inanimate objects.
>
> "What's come over the child?" The people exchanged glances. And the very same question seemed to stare from the eyes of the lover himself.
>
> For a long time they went on looking at her. But her face gave nothing away. A sickly light seemed to shine from it. And then this light, too, died away and her face grew cold.
>
> "Shall we go out for a walk this evening?" asked Shutz.
>
> "Where to?" she said, and the words sounded less like a question than a harsh statement of fact.   (109, 10)

The passage begins with the falling of darkness and with silence. Again silence is evoked as a lack or absence: "and the words died away." The words have died the way people might die, indeed, the way the Jews of Badenheim will die—as a final and permanent eclipse of body and of soul, of life, and of the traces of that life in the world. We hear the dying of those words, that is, we hear their absence in the spaces they once occupied. And in that newly emptied space, a woman is curled up in her covers like a caterpillar in its cocoon, like a swaddled child. The interchange of the characters who worry over her and then suggest taking a walk is domestic and familiar. But things are far from ordinary, and the effect of the scene bears this out. The guests communicate an alarm to us in the looks that they exchange. And the most commonplace and amiable of questions, "Shall we go out for a walk this evening?" brings another question in its wake, a question that points to the restrictions on movement that now govern the lives of the Jews of Badenheim: "Where to?"

Appelfeld relates not only the question that the schoolgirl tosses back to her concerned lover, but also its sound: "and the words sounded less like a question than a harsh statement of fact." The timbre of the words reveals all that her words cannot. The receding of outer and inner light, and the dying of words and of expression in the child's face, give way to a place in which questions have narrowed into facts. And fact is indeed all that the Jews of Badenheim cannot name or confront. It is the knowledge that has so drastically transformed the schoolgirl, a knowledge that is feared, suspected, denied, and shared by the Jews of Badenheim, even as it remains unspoken.

The Demotion of Words and Narrative

Within the aesthetics of literary texts that take historical horror as their subject, there is a demotion of words and narrative from their functions of signifying, sequencing, ordering, and telling. At the same time the aesthetic properties and balances created by the words and narrative, its "voicing," becomes paramount. Marlow's obsession with Kurtz's voice tells us that the real story with which Marlow is concerned cannot not be told in narrative form at all. It will be "voiced" just as Appelfeld's description of the dying of words in rooms that anticipate the absence of the people who sit in them "voices" the fate that cannot be addressed explicitly or directly.

On the level of the words they use and their meanings, the Jews of Badenheim are utterly naive. They never suspect that "relocation to Poland" is anything other than resettlement. But Appelfeld manages to give them words that maintain a tacit silence while the same words are shot through with an ironic candor and humor, one which relies on the informed position of the reader while leaving ambiguous just how much or how little the speaker herself suspects. As the deportation draws closer, music rehearsals are more frequent:

The nights were now high and transparent. The hotel throbbed to the sounds of music. Even the laziest of musicians practiced. No one could say anymore: "Why don't you rehearse?" Never before had Badenheim heard such a concentration of sounds.

"Isn't that a feast for the ear!" exclaimed Dr. Pappen-heim.

"They're driving me crazy," grumbled Mitzi.

"You wouldn't like us to appear in Poland unre-hearsed, would you? What would people say?"   (111)

Trude, the pharmacist's mad wife, confides to her hus-band: "Soon we'll go to Poland and all will be well." Memo-ries fill her and her words. She speaks of the Poland she remembers from childhood and of Yiddish, the language of the Jews of Poland:

When she spoke about Poland her eyes lit up, and the sorrow was erased from her brow. A new, young skin seemed to be growing over her face. She laughed.

Martin asked many questions. "Are the rivers in Poland beautiful?"

And Trude spared no details. There was no country as beautiful as Poland, no air as pure as Polish air.

"And Yiddish? You know I don't speak Yiddish."

"There's nothing easier than learning Yiddish. It's a simple, beautiful language, and Polish too is a beautiful language."   (118)

Poland is a word that releases all sorts of feelings and asso-ciations with family, with origins, with the Jewish identity that the assimilated Jews of Badenheim long ago discarded. At the same time, descriptions of rehearsals that will go on in Poland and references to the purity of the air in Poland are elliptical ref-erences to death camps and extermination. The characters are thus endlessly elaborating a coded way of speaking their feel-ings, thoughts, and ideas about their fate while respecting the taboo against their more direct articulation.

When, in a similar vein, we are told that Dr. Pappenheim has carefully chosen the words with which he describes the future to another of the guests, those words register at one and the same time as the coded speech of a knowing man and as the ironic speech of an utterly naive man:

> "In a few days' time everything will change. We are on the threshold of a radical change," said Pappenheim, choosing his words with great deliberation.   (112)

And he continues enigmatically a couple of paragraphs later, "There are many Jews living in Poland. In the last analysis, a man has to return to his origins" (112).

The ambiguity here of such a pointed utterance that is pathetically naive and daringly knowing, that denies on one level that which, on another level, is acknowledged, even accepted, is a way of addressing the nature of genocide as the Jews of Badenheim experience it. To know somewhere deep down and yet be unable to integrate that knowing, to need to speak and yet not to speak, to speak around, to speak in coded ways that do not intrude upon this silence, tells us more about the experience of historical horror than words possibly could.

The Jews of Badenheim use the word Poland—the site of their extermination to come—in order to suggest that their deportation is merely a kind of emigration and hence, really, a form of rescue. Theirs is an informal, if unconscious, conspiracy of speakers, not to represent but to misrepresent. Beyond all that is implicit in such an effort, we come to experience words (and, more broadly speaking, narrative) not in their adequacy, but in their inadequacy; not for their ability to name their object, but in their helplessness before it.

Appelfeld does not name the thing that cannot be named. He never, ultimately, provides us with a word or image that pretends to correspond to the grievous experience he is seeking to communicate. Instead he brings us words, images, and symbols that betray to us their inability to establish the kind of simple equation of word for thing we take for granted as speakers. In this way, the silence is never broken. It is only made more palpable.

And Appelfeld is quite explicit in his sense of how a traumatic historical experience interjects itself between words and their meanings:

> Words without bodies floated in the lobby . . .
>   The words did not seem to belong to the present. They were words of the spring which had somehow lingered on, suspended in the void.   (117)

In this strange and strangely moving metaphor, Appelfeld tells us that something has come apart. Words have been sundered from their bodies. They are no longer rooted in the objects and world they are intended to represent. Instead they float in the hotel lobby like the lost souls of the Homeric underworld. It is as though there has been a rupture of an original and living wholeness of words, their speakers, and the world they speak of. With that rupture, people lack the words they need to describe their experience of the world, to make that world coherent, if not less awful, and to situate themselves in it. Like the schoolgirl, the Jews of Badenheim do not go out for walks. They retreat from the sunshine to the hotel and to the anger, fear, and confusion that cripple them, and at the same time, shield them from truths too terrible to acknowledge:

> If not for the angry people it would have been possible to take a stroll to the square and enjoy the coolness in the air. The sun was still shining, but the angry people clung stubbornly to the old words, hoarding them like antiquated gadgets that had gone out of use. Since they were unable to liberate themselves from the old words and the fear, they prowled the streets and cast their angry shadows.   (115)

All of us understand this silence. We understand that this silence is not a picture, a symbol, a "representation," but a literal lack of words for something very actual and real. Silence is part of the traumatic experience in the same way that paralysis of a limb is a part of polio. And if polio is as severe as the paralysis that accompanies it, we might say that an experience is traumatic to the extent that it cannot be put into words.

This simple human calculation is essential to the aesthetic organization and effect of the novel. The reader intuitively assesses the intensity of struggle surrounding the effort to find words. The portrait of historical horror is accomplished in the accumulation and organization of a host of detail, all of which touch upon silence: the rich portrait of human speechlessness, the way in which a poeticized and symbolic surface of the novel reinforces that speechlessness, the felt disparities between words and their meanings, the rhetorical axis of desire for speech upon which the portrait of silence and its poignance turn, the image of music that is both a symbol of this desire and an ironic formulation of its disappointment.

Badenheim 1939 is organized in a very elaborate and detailed way around a convention in rhetoric that is among the oldest and that, at the same time, is a commonplace of speech at its most ordinary. Before the recounting of wonderful, terrifying or extraordinary events, Virgil, like Homer, before him and Dante after, prefaces his description with a demurral: "Words cannot describe . . . ," the poet tells us. This assertion, that words cannot tell, describe, express, communicate, represent, or convey a particular event, is itself a means of gesturing to that which is experienced as being beyond words.

Unlike his ancient and medieval predecessors, Appelfeld does not immediately follow such a protest with a blow-by-blow description of the incredible experience he wishes to relate. Appelfeld makes this simple rhetorical gesture, not a preface to his tale, but its substance. The Festival is continually at risk because the tools of expression, be they words or music, are problematic. Shortly after Pappenheim receives an order to register all of his musicians with the Sanitation Department, the Festival collapses. Music, a symbol in its wordlessness of all that words cannot express, is no longer possible. Concerts cease. We are told that a child prodigy, the "yanuka," has lost his voice and grown fat. And what does the story of a music festival have to do with the story of the deportation of the Jews of Badenheim, anyway? The absurd counterpointing of the deportation process with the fortunes of a music festival projects the longings and the inadequacies of human speech into the fabric of the novel.

Susan Shapiro, in a philosophical discussion of the incomplete ways we listen to testimony of catastrophic events, connects the possibility of speech, language, coherence, and thought itself to social existence, which it is the point of genocide to destroy, utterly and irrevocably. "The Holocaust ruptured," Shapiro writes:

> . . . those primary social relations and functions, such as friendship, family, loyalty and even the very desire to live, that, as *sensus communis*, underlie and found coherent speech itself. The rupture of language is, thus, not incidental, but central to the radically negative character of the event. The negating character of the event cannot be understood, therefore, as either external or occasional to thought. Rather, it must be recognized as a negation already present in our language, in that which conditions and makes possible thought.[4]

The unrepresentability, silence, and negation of which Shapiro writes is precisely the symbolic and thematic heart of the novel. And Appelfeld writes this negation or silence in a manner consistent with the nature of that negation—contrapuntally and ironically. As the extermination draws closer, what flickers of hope remain, cluster around the Festival itself:

> The drugs ran out and the people sank into themselves, into their sadness. Despair now stared from every wall. The kitchen was dark, the tea tables were deserted, and the two chandeliers hung askew, like the morning after a wild party. What could be done? If only the Festival could be revived!   (133)

The Festival signifies the desire for expression that is frustrated and raised in its urgency to the desperation of the life urge itself. And its fortunes become an intimate chronicle of an inner breakdown that afflicts Dr. Pappenheim, his artists, the hotel guests, and their uninvited Jewish guests who are fated to join them in their struggle. At this point in the novel, the trains that will whisk Badenheim's Jews to their fate are seven chapters away. Food is less plentiful in the hotel. Martin's pharmacy has been looted several times over, once for its poisons, later for drugs and cosmetics. The musicians have accumulated fortunes by robbing the hotel of its silver and fine china; they consume chocolate in secret, nightly feasts that bring them fear but no joy. The hotel population has increased beyond its paying guests as Jews who have been removed from their homes in different towns and villages are sent to await deportation at the hotel.

After Dr. Pappenheim receives notice that all of his artists are to be placed at the disposal of the Sanitation Department, the Festival falls apart. On a literal level this is a function of the extermination process that is imminently to destroy Pappenheim's musicians. On another level altogether, the silencing of the Festival and of its musicians is about the silencing of formal expression altogether and thus about the silence within language and of language that is, in Shapiro's words, "central to the negating character of the event" of the Holocaust. Aesthetically, it is this "silencing of forms" that makes possible our hearing of that other silence, by its radical and historical nature, more awful, more forbidding, more difficult to discern: that silence in history for which there are no forms or means of expression.

The falling apart of the Festival collapses the destruction of bodies and the destruction of forms into one another. It is as though, to hear a silence in history, Appelfeld had first to pick away at language and words and the screens they provide in the very act of naming. Pappenheim's announcement of the collapse of the Festival is pathetic, zany, surreal, and terrible all at once:

> Dr. Pappenheim stood at the hotel gates and held forth to the strangers. Someone asked for information about the Festival. Pappenheim apologized for the confusion in the schedule. He had done everything in his

power, but what could he do if this year other matters had taken precedence?

If only the Festival could be revived! Was there no way in which the Festival could be revived? The people now dogged Dr. Pappenheim's footsteps not with demands but with pleas. The drug they had become accustomed to over the years, it was this drug they now craved above all. Dr. Pappenheim stood by the great artist's door and begged: "just one concert, just one, have mercy on us. . . ."   (134)

The image of Pappenheim standing at the gates of the hotel, and then by the door of his guest artist, Mandelbaum, imploring him to have mercy and perform "just one concert, just one" touches the raw psychic nerve of Appelfeld's trapped human beings. The passage is striking for its gentle mockery of Pappenheim's all but inarticulate plea in the face of an overwhelming fate about to overtake him, his artists, and the rest of the Jews of Badenheim. Gesture and power of expression fail the good maestro who stands at the gates of the city and holds forth to strangers in the pose, Appelfeld tells us, of the ancient prophets of Israel whose words have the wings, the power, the wrath of God that he so utterly lacks. The preoccupation with food, the stealing of china and cutlery, and the scrambling for drugs in the novel all follow from the impossibility of ordering experience and feeling, whether in words, in music, or in action, in ways that address the fate hanging over the Jews of Badenheim. Like Pappenheim's misdirected cry for mercy and his worry about schedules, the breakdown of manners in *Badenheim 1939* is another sign of an essential speechlessness that afflicts the characters of the novel. And where words cannot be found, the reader is then involved in apprehending, not words, but their failure and the silences produced by that failure.

Two Modes of Silence

Pappenheim's condition of speechlessness takes shape against another silence, a silence that has found its form and for which the Festival and music itself are symbols. Appelfeld's description of the twins who recite Rilke's death sonnets crystallizes the possibilities of expression upon which the novel turns:

> The moment they ascended the stage their emaciation took on a compelling power. Their mastery was such that the words did not seem like words at all; they were as pure and abstract as if they had never been touched by human mouths.
>
> For a whole hour they stood there on the stage in total concentration. And by the end of the hour the words did their work alone, flying through the air like birds on fire.   (101)

The novel seeks words that fly "through the air like birds on fire," and brings us, instead, words that float "in the void like tired, dispirited birds." Rilke's poetic articulation of death and its meanings brings late romantic, lyrical and mystic notions of poesis into the novel while the actual fabric of Appelfeld's narration uses words in ways that remind us of how different they are from the things they are supposed to evoke.

The Rilkean paradigm presents a view of language, of art, and of the possibility of expression that falls apart in Badenheim along with one of the favorite symbolist metaphors, that of music for a desired order that is utterly beyond expression. The idea of music, a central theme of *Badenheim 1939*, brings a religious vocabulary of desire and transcendence into the novel against which another silence makes itself heard, a silence in which words cannot come together, cannot sing.

In an article by Gisele Brelet included by Suzanne Langer in her *Reflections on Art*, Brelet analyzes the relationship of silence to music:[5]

> Sound is an event: by its coming it breaks an original silence, and it ends in a final silence. And music, like sound, projects its form upon a background of silence which it always presupposes. Music is born, develops,

and realizes itself within silence: upon silence it traces
out its moving arabesques, which give form to silence,
and yet do not abolish it. . . .   (103)

Brelet is interested in music as a becoming, as an event, and in
silence as a calm "far from the world of matter and space which
noises symbolize," in which "those who listen no longer hear
anything but the voice of their inwardness" (103). And she iden-
tifies music with silence because silence contains the "possibility of all sounds."

If sound seems to surge forth from silence, it is because
it cannot in fact be born except from the movement by
which, in silence, activity was already orienting itself
towards the making of sound.   (105)

Badenheim 1939 plays with the idea of that silence that is a com-
ponent of music and artistic expression and with another silence
that is as different from it as noise is from a melodic phrase.

When food supplies do not arrive at the hotel and the headwaiter goes to the storeroom of the hotel, his fingers tremble "as
if the treasures of the world to come had suddenly been revealed
to him." The imagery of the passage is explicitly religious. The
headwaiter first "illuminates the darkness with a flashlight."
Light brings revelation. The headwaiter is struck with the perception of a plenitude, which is like treasures from "the world to
come." And Appelfeld describes the feelings aroused in the
headwaiter as feelings that are religious and reverential. "'From
here?' asked the headwaiter reverentially" (103).

If the religious language of the passage suggests fulfillment
and promises a coming together of feeling and of words, such an
event does not occur. The flashlight reveals only "a big room full
of antique furniture," and the passage ends with Appelfeld's
description of a very different silence that is found in the storeroom: "the kind of silence only found in sealed-off places hung
congealed in the air" (103).

The silence of spiritual essence and fulfillment of which
Brelet writes is the ironic ground out of which this different and

diminished silence articulates itself. We sense the disjunction of these two kinds of silence as Appelfeld continues his description of the headwaiter and his joy:

> The headwaiter was as happy as if he had been pro-moted. The hotel was now full of the fragrant aromas of liquors, Swiss chocolate, French wine, pecans, and fine peach preserves. The people sat at the tables and ate with quiet enjoyment.
>
> "This is a time we'll remember forever," exulted the musician Zimbelman.   (103)

The passage employs gestures and language of promise in order to move, not to a variety of levels of opening, but to a strangely restricted form of fulfillment, that of people eating at the table. The quiet of the people is part of a paralysis we recognize on a narrative level. The ticking off of a list of fine luxury foods—the liquors, Swiss chocolate, French wine, pecans, and peach jelly—leaves us without the sense of eating as a socially connecting act, but as a concession to appetites that continue to hunger for another kind of fulfillment, one that is not so much as whispered.

The last sentence is especially pointed in the biting, tongue-in-cheek manner so characteristic of Appelfeld. "This is a time we'll remember forever," Zimbelman exults, continuing the religious imagery of the passage and referring to memory in the face of a future that promises only deportation, death, and the obliteration of memory. Indeed, the image of the exulting musician completes a description of happiness that should in its sensory, emotive, and symbolic meanings point away from the sealed storeroom, but that, instead, spins directly out of the congealed silence of the storeroom.

In Yiddish, *Zimbelman* means "man of cymbals," an instrument that is prominent in classical Hebrew descriptions of the angels, their music, and, especially, of music in its aspect of power. The meaning of the name underlines the powerlessness of the character in his historical situation, the powerlessness of his musical vocabulary and of the silence that longs for, but cannot find, the fulfillment that it seeks.

Image and Symbol: The Textures of Silence

Badenheim 1939 brings a stripped prose to bear upon a symbolic fabric of longing and desire. Within that fabric, music is symbolic of the wordless, of beyondness, of silence, and of realization in language that is continually disappointed. The sounds of silence are everywhere heard along with the longing for essence and fulfillment that they bring. But silence stumbles on silence of another kind, as in the beautifully articulated tones of the closing sentence in the following passage:

> And in the evening Martin gave them tea and cookies. It was like old times. Helena took the peasant shawl off her head and her high forehead transmitted a dry sorrow. She stirred her tea and the sounds died down one after another.   (136)

The articulation of this other, diminished silence depends upon the disappointing of a variety of rhetorical, stylistic, and other cues along with a powerful evocation of the lyrical and mystical silence of which music is a symbol. The impact of this juxtaposition is one of texture. It lies in the juxtapositioning of the stuckness of the one with the flow and connectedness of the other, the play of image against symbol.

As much as music is a symbol of expressiveness, it is symbolic of the idea of symbol itself. As such, the silence of music is part of the numinous, of a deeper reality within a system of correspondences. Its texture is flowing, mysterious, evocative. But as image, silence in *Badenheim 1939* is cut from a very different fabric. Its texture is not numinous but dense, heavy, even viscous; a silence that extends out of, but not past, the traumatic condition. Image and symbol provide a dialogue of unsatisfactory alternatives and a tension out of which Appelfeld makes palpable the experience of historical horror. At one point Appelfeld describes the atmosphere in the hotel:

> The rustle of paper was no longer heard in the hotel. The silence was dense and from day to day it grew denser.
> (70)

After an angry outburst by one character, the silence that follows is described in this way:

> In the end he withdrew his head and a heavy silence
> descended with the darkness and enfolded the people
> huddled in the corners of the lobby.   (142)

And as the summer stretches toward fall and the deportation grows closer, the hotel guests more exhausted, Appelfeld describes the nighttime silence that the dogs pierce with their shrieking as though it were a vulnerable object among other surrounding objects in the world:

> The dogs could not understand what was happening.
> The angry glare in their eyes shone like polished metal.
> And at night they tore the silence to shreds.   (139)

Silence in its opacity, its vulnerability, its lack of transparence, suggests something that is impenetrable and incomprehensible. It is a silence that reverberates on other levels as well, for example in the comment of a waiter in the hotel about his guests: "If I could serve them Rilke's Death sonnets maybe they would eat. It seems they can't digest any other food" (36).

The trapped Jews of Badenheim cannot digest their situation. They hunger for the words that will bring comprehension to their condition, express what they cannot express, and lift the awful silence around them. They hunger for Pappenheim's music festival and for the cry of Mandelbaum's violin whose "clean polished notes" are able to "cut through the silence" (87). But the clarity they seek holds terror as well:

> That very night Mandelbaum shut himself up in his
> room: the clean, polished notes cut through the silence.
> Now a new fear fell on the people: Mandelbaum.   (87)

The terror, of course, could hardly be more real. To move out of a condition of silence to the silence of a beyondness named, a terror acknowledged, despair given voice, is a temptation, a dilemma, but not, finally, a possibility.

Chapter 3

Silence in Language and in History

> Now the Sirens have a still more fatal weapon than their song, namely their silence.
>
> —*Franz Kafka*

In his study of silence, Bernard P. Dauenhauer describes the relationship of language and silence this way:

> Therefore originary and fundamental silence is not the contrary of language. Rather than being that which thwarts language, silence is that which opens the way for language's potency . . . for speech is born from silence and seeks its conclusion in silence. This is the case because there is in principle an exchange between experience and language. Neither is closed within itself.[1]

The notion of an "exchange between experience and language" and the emphasis upon a dynamic between the two describe a system of relations that exist within literary works whose subject falls within the range of the familiar and credible. The traumatic historical experience disrupts this "exchange between experience and language" since trauma itself includes a loss of words. Such experiences create impassable rifts between the domain of experience and that of language, and bring into hearing a very different set of silences that follow from the breakdown of the relationship Dauenhauer describes.

The pages that follow begin with a more detailed exploration of the open relationship Dauenhauer traces between language and experience and the kinds of silences that enter into that relationship. This discussion precedes the real focus of this chapter, which is on the breakdown of this dynamic—a breakdown I examine in works by Claude Lanzmann, André Schwarz-Bart, Jerzy Kosinski, Tadeusz Borowski and Paul Celan—that occurs in works of historical horror, works that fall on the "far" side of representational limit. Works of historical horror tend to juxtapose these two above-mentioned silences against one another; silences that arise within the Dauenhauer dynamic give way, under the pressure of the traumatic experience, to very different silences that arise with the breakdown of that dynamic.

The silence of historical horror is, then, a silence that longs for articulation, for the potencies and seductions of words, at the same time that it is the contrary of language. It is a silence that repeatedly thwarts language, overwhelms it, and speaks, not by naming or telling stories, but through devices of omission, substitution, inference, and irony, as well as by telling its own story: the story of the desire for, and of the breaking down, of speech. If Dauenhauer describes silences that arise within a poetic of the representable, this chapter and the preceding one are concerned with elucidating a different, more complicated continuum of silence, one that arises and stammers within a poetic of the unrepresentable.

Silence within a Poetic of Representability

Dauenhauer writes that the silence that precedes speech is a silence that calls language forth, that "opens the way for language's potency. . . ." Rainer Maria Rilke in "The First Elegy" of his *Duino Elegies*, uses the notion of silence in precisely this sense. He admonishes his heart to listen deeply to the silence out of which emerges meaning:

> But listen to the voice of the wind and the
>   ceaseless message that forms itself
>   out of silence.
> It is murmuring toward you now from those who die
>   young.[2]

It is precisely the silence of the world of experience, history, and death that liberates the word. "Man arrives at speech," wrote the Hebrew poet Haim Nahman Bialik, "out of the magnitude of his fear of remaining even one moment in the abyss, face to face with unmediated nothingness." Similarly, in the last lines of the elegy, Rilke refers to the absence created by death as a "startled space." The song of the poet fills the space or void that "felt for the first time/ that harmony which now enraptures and comforts and helps us."[3]

The "exchange between language and experience" here is one that consoles, assuages pain, and, indeed, brings rapture in the wake of loss. In her study of music and silence, Giselle Brelet explains the crucial relationship between absence and presence:

> The spiritual act only awakens in the absence of its object, and from that initial deprivation is born its movement towards its object. . . . Everyone knows with what intensity an object or being materially absent can be present in our imagination. It is the very nature of the mind to make of absence the instrument of presence.[4]

The spiritual act—in Rilke's case, the poetic act—cannot take place except through the promptings of painful losses. This understanding of the relationship of silence to speech, of experience to language, is deeply embedded in language itself. ". . . for speech is born from silence and seeks its conclusion in silence," Dauenhauer writes, pointing to another dimension of silence, to a silence that is the goal of speech and which is produced by speech. "The word," Max Picard writes in *World of Silence* "not only brings the things out of silence; it also produces the silence in which they can disappear again."[5]

George Steiner observes some of the connections between language, transcendence and silence. In a detailed consideration of the final cantos of Dante's *Paradiso*, he shows how the repeated assertion of a failure of words is the mechanism by which transcendence makes itself felt:

> But it is decisively the fact that language does have its frontiers . . . which gives proof of a transcendent presence in the fabric of the world. It is just because we can go no further, because speech so marvelously fails us, that we experience the certitude of a divine meaning surpassing and enfolding ours. What lies beyond man's word is eloquent of God.[6]

Steiner is suggesting that a rhetoric of transcendence depends precisely upon the experience (and thereby also a rhetoric) of limit. In evoking and pressing against that limit, we move from known to unknown, from a world of contingency to what Hermann Broch in *The Death of Virgil* called "the word beyond speech":

> The word hovered over the universe, over the nothing, floating beyond the expressible as well as the inexpressible, and he, caught under and amidst the roaring, he floated on with the word . . . , it was the word beyond speech.[7]

The passage is especially interesting because it describes language as unfixed and floating. Man flows with the word toward the "word beyond speech." Within that process, the speaker moves from a silence in the world to a deeper silence. In the words of Max Picard:

It is as though behind silence were the absolute word to which, through silence, human language moves. It is as though the human word were sustained by the absolute word. . . . Silence is like a remembrance of that word.[8]

The sensibility of the modern period articulates itself precisely around this transaction that moves from silence in the world to deeper silence, that accomplishes the leap from limit to transcendence that Steiner describes. The crucial influence is Mallarmé who "came to realize that the logos—God's expression—was beyond the human, and could not be heard or apprehended, for it was silence, the absolute, source of all things."[9] He hears the silence that is produced by speech and aims at the evocation, not of things but of the deeper silence behind those things:

I say: flower—and out of the oblivion into which my voice consigns every contour, apart from the known calyxes, there arises musically, the idea itself, the flower absent from all bouquets.[10]

Both modern and postmodern periods privilege the question of that leap, how to accomplish it and whether it is possible in the first place. The poetic project of Wallace Stevens is devoted to the question of how to move from the "absence in reality" of "things as they are" to the "rhapsody of things as they are."[11]

As modernity wears on, the transaction of world and word becomes a project of increasing difficulty and the silence articulated, a silence of failed transcendence. "The fact is," Eugene Ionesco wrote in his diaries, "that words say nothing, if I may put it that way. . . . There are no words for the deepest experience. . . ."[12] And if the deepest experience cannot be reclaimed by speech, the world itself and its humblest objects reveal, for Samuel Beckett, the gap that separates consciousness from the world, names from things. The protagonist of Samuel Beckett's *Watt* looks at that affable, dependable, and necessary item, a pot, and thinks:

"it was not a pot, the more he looked, the more he reflected, the more he felt sure of that, that it was not a pot at all. It resembled a pot, it was almost a pot, but it was not a pot of which one could say, Pot, pot and be comforted."[13]

Beckett and Ionesco question the dynamic that Dauenhauer describes even as they write from within that dynamic. But the problem of finding names for things that is the burden of Watt's soliloquy on a pot is of a different nature than the problem of finding names for things in *Badenheim 1939* where the Jews awaiting their extermination are increasingly at a loss for words to describe the destruction awaiting them. In *At the Mind's Limit*, Jean Améry, the Belgian social philosopher who spent a year in Auschwitz, distinguishes between modern forms of philosophical nihilism and his own experience:

> It is not Being that oppresses me, or Nothingness, or God, or the Absence of God, only society. For it and only it caused the disturbance in my existential balance, which I am trying to oppose with an upright gait. It and only it robbed me of my trust in the world.[14]

In the tracing of a collapse of the "exchange between experience and language" in works of historical horror and the sealing off of each into their separate domains, a very different set of silences makes itself heard against the more familiar set of silences Dauenhauer describes. These silences involve, simultaneously, events in language and in history: a silence of language created by this "collapse" and the silence of historical and traumatic experience that speaks by virtue of and "across" this collapse and its fissures.

The Marking and Opening Up of Historical Silence

Claude Lanzmann's film, *Shoah*, is concerned with the fact of massive death and with the denial and resistances that surround and defend against a knowledge of that fact.[15] The passage below follows a familiar rhetorical pattern. The eyewitness and survivor repeatedly asserts that what he saw cannot be described and is beyond belief.[16] Except that his goal is not rhetorical.[17] The speaker is describing his own existential plight of remembering as he stands on the physical location of the death camp forty years later. If the assertion in Danté brings us closer to transcendence, the assertion here brings us closer to a historical chaos that, like God, is outside language:

> There were two huge ovens. It was terrible. No one can describe it. No one can recreate what happened here. Impossible? And no one can understand it. Even I, here, now. I can't believe I'm here. No, I just can't believe it. It was always this peaceful here. Always. When they burned 2000 people—Jews—every day, it was just as peaceful. No one shouted. . . . It was silent. Peaceful. Just as it is now. . . .   (16)

The effort begins in the first sentence with the mention of the crematoria. The speaker interrupts his description of the killing for a space of eight sentences, in which he speaks of the impossibility of communicating, or even of believing, the events to which he was witness forty years earlier. The last four sentences divide their attention between the killing and the quiet of the landscape. The quiet of the landscape seems to involve nature in a resistance to the horror of mass extermination at the same time that it is a tangible reminder of those very events: "It was silent. Peaceful. Just as it is now. . . ."

There is a struggle around silence that comes across in the passage above, which is the subject of Lanzmann's film. As Lanzmann presses eyewitness after eyewitness for details of their experiences, speech repeatedly breaks down. The absence of those killed and the factuality of mass killing accumulate as those killed acquire the faces of neighbor, brother, cousin, mother, father, child, husband, and wife. Lanzmann repeatedly has to step in and coax his witness to face his memory, his pain, his knowledge, his resistance. With each attempt to press his witnesses to find words, Lanzmann brings into view the terrible breach in the transaction described by Dauenhauer, between domains of experience and domains of expression, a transaction whose unraveling we witness on the film before our very eyes, again and again.

In order to hear a silence in history, Lanzmann presents us with a resistance to language itself. As stories fall apart and as we witness the enactment of a literal, and not merely rhetorical, failure of the word, we begin to hear that other silence in all of its historical depth, chaos, and horror. Lanzmann, at another point in the film, foregrounds yet another silence linked to history, one that is the physical mark of the killing process.

In the excerpt that follows, Lanzmann picks up the word *silence* which a witness, the Sobibor railway switchman, Jan Piwonski, uses to describe the sudden quiet that revealed the gassing of several thousand Jews the previous night, a night that initiated the exterminations at Sobibor. Lanzmann questions Piwonski about that silence:

> The next morning . . . the station was absolutely silent, and we realized after talking with the other railway men who worked at the station here, that something utterly incomprehensible had happened. First of all, when the camp was being built there were orders shouted in German, there were screams, Jews were working at a run, there were shots, and here there was that silence, no work crews, a really total silence. Forty cars had arrived, and then . . . nothing. It was all very strange.
>
> **It was the silence that tipped them off?**
>
> That's right.
>
> **Can he describe that silence?**
>
> It was a silence . . . a standstill in the camp. You heard and saw nothing; nothing moved. So then they began to wonder, "Where have they put those Jews?"   (67)

This silence that Piwonski describes is the direct consequence of the previous night's extermination, as well as Piwonski's clue in sense datum experience to what had transpired. His discovery begins with hearing and seeing: "You heard and saw nothing; nothing moved," he says. The mind then begins to make its connections: "So then they began to wonder, "Where have they put those Jews?"

If the killing process has a beginning, middle, and end, the end is precisely the silence that Piwonski and other workers hear in the camp for the first time. It is evidence of the unbelievable—testimony to historical horror. Lanzmann calls attention to the event of that silence and to the nature of its connection to the killing as a way of pointing to radical and inadmissible aspects of human existence. To dwell on the silence that is linked to the killing process, that is the very mark of the killing process, is to dwell precisely on the unintegratable and traumatic fact, and hence to begin to hear a silence profoundly resisted and, therefore, profoundly silent, at the chaotic heart of history.

The artistic strategy of the film is precisely to work against all the devices in art, in language, in the human mind, that interfere with, take us away from, and obscure that reality. Lanzmann stages history before us. That is, he places the memory of an experience before our eyes in the persons of eyewitnesses whom he has flown to the very locations of their remembering all over Europe. We witness the impact of their experiences in their words, on their faces, and in their voices. He includes shots of the camera filming his witnesses in order to authenticate and verify the witnessing of his witnesses and the procedures of his gathering that testimony. In this way, Lanzmann's film attempts to exchange, for the pretenses of art and its special claims to represent the real, another kind of link and transaction with the real, a link of witnessing in which the viewer is witness to the witness.[18]

Lanzmann's technique echoes essential elements of Conrad's *Heart of Darkness*. The revelation of horror in Conrad as in the Lanzmann film is personal, intimate, and involves a chain of witnesses: Kurtz, Marlow, Marlow's sea friends to whom he spins out his tale, and the reader who overhears the tale.[19] The credibility of Kurtz's whispered communication depends, as in

Lanzmann's film, on the authority of personal experience—
experience that is excluded from the narrative at the same time
that it marks the voice in which it is told. Marlow undertakes his
journey into the African depths for the sake, not of Kurtz's stories, but to hear his voice: "The man presented himself as a
voice. . . ."[20] Marlow tells us, and at another point remembers
Kurtz as, "A voice! A voice! It rang deep to the very last . . ." (69).

We listen, in *Shoah*, not to the stories told, but to the voices
in which these stories are told, or, more often, not told. Works of
historical horror repeatedly focus on the breakdown of the relationship between experience and language, the silence of and
within language that follows in the wake of that breakdown,
and, finally, upon the human voice itself and the ways it is
marked by its experiences. The marks of traumatic historical
experience, then, if not lexically available, are audible in the
voice that is our venue, finally, to the silence outside language.

Silence, Articulation, and History

The breakdown of an "exchange between experience and
language" implicates a world that lies outside this exchange and
outside the formal enterprise itself as Dauenhauer describes it.
Thus far we have examined two sets of silences, silence that
arises within language and therefore within a poetic of representability and silence that occurs outside such a poetic, outside
representational limit and language altogether. "The Tower," a
poem by the poet, survivor, and scholar of medieval Hebrew
poetry, Dan Pagis, is about both kinds of silences.[21] We have seen
how Claude Lanzmann in his film *Shoah* tries to bring us closer
to that contradiction in terms, a silence outside language, mind,
and representation. If the eloquence of *Shoah* lies precisely in the
breakdown of the narratives of Lanzmann's witnesses, the
poem by Pagis is, conversely, a narrative of that breakdown. As
in Conrad's *Heart of Darkness*, it is about the before and after of
an articulation that cannot take place. It is a study of kinds of
silence: of the silence that "opens the way for language's
potency" and of a silence that cannot be voiced because it is out-

side language. And it is about the conflicted relationship of these silences, the deeper problematic of language and traumatic experience that underlies this conflict.

The Tower

1	I did not want to grow, but quick-fingered memories
2	put layer upon layer, each one alone,
3	and were mixed in the tumult of strange
4	tongues and left in me unguarded entrances,
5	stairs that led nowhere,
6	perspectives that were broken.
7	Finally, I was abandoned.
8	Only sometimes in the twisted corridor
9	a small speechless whisper
10	still rises in me and runs
11	like a draft and it seems to me
12	that I am a whirlwind
13	whose head is for a moment in the sky
14	and before I wake up
15	the mess of my burnt bricks crumbles
16	and turns back
17	to clay. (89)

The poem tells of an elusive moment in which memory and desire mingle in the self, the very moment in which "the exchange between experience and language" takes place. It follows this exchange in time. The first seven lines of the poem are written in the past tense, and outline the effect of experience upon memory. In the next six lines, the poet speaks of the effort to articulate experience in a present tense that is filled with the tenuous perception of a whisper that "still rises in me," and with the tentative hope that makes it seem "to me that I am a whirlwind . . ." (8–13). The final four lines of the poem tell of the effect of experience on language in the crumbling of the tower, a breakdown that occurs in the present tense from a precisely delineated point in time that is described as the moment before awakening (14–17). The poem, then, moves along a temporal path toward the constriction and collapse that are implicit in the crumbling of the tower.

Pagis employs traditional devices of poetic language to describe an untraditional situation in which those devices, and the impulse out of which they arise, founder and fall apart. The tower—or "migdal" in the original Hebrew—refers to a self that lives in the world and accumulates the memories of its experiences in that world. At the same time it is also a reference to "migdal Bavel," the tower of Babel built by Noah's descendants in their attempt to reach heaven, an attempt for which the tower is destroyed and the human and linguistic confusions of a multiplicity of languages is established on earth. Historical memory in the poem involves a post-Babel situation: memories are "mixed in the tumult of strange tongues." The self cannot draw upon its past and experiences in the charting of a future or vision: the memories leave "stairs that led nowhere,/ perspectives that were broken" (5, 6). It is here in this tower that symbolizes self, memory, transcendence, and language, that the exchange of which Dauenhauer writes between experience and language, between a remembering "I" and a poetic "I," takes place.

The silence in which "a small speechless whisper/ still rises in me . . ." (9), is the very silence and longing that "opens the way for language's potency." For a brief moment the silence of the "speechless whisper," of an impulse that is yet "bli omer," without word, but which seeks the word, moves into the foreground. The whisper, which itself is a flow of air out of the body, is figured in highly traditional literary terms as wind. It is referred to first as a draft, and then as a whirlwind (11, 12). Like the welter of experience out of which it rises, the impulse is disconnected from its deep creative and life sources: it arises in a "twisted corridor" (8) of the self and it arises "sometimes" (8), that is, fitfully, unbidden and against the better knowledge of "stairs that led nowhere" (5) and of "perspectives that were broken" (6).

In the silence and space in which the impulse arises, the self becomes aware of a direction. If the whisper is still without word, the goal of those words is sensed as an upward motion in which the speechless whisper first arises, gathers a certain amount of energy until it runs through the tower "like a draft," perceiving itself finally as fully energized in the form of a "whirlwind/ whose head is for a moment in the sky" (11, 12, 13). The flow described in Pagis's poem takes the self from the dismembered chaos of its experience in the world to a very different locus in the world in which the self might also touch the sky or transcend. Significantly, we have descriptions of self and of language that are similar to the flow that Broch describes toward "the word beyond speech."

But the open space of a silence within, a silence that is fraught with desire for articulation and fueled by a silence outside the self and in the world, cannot arrive at the deeper silence that is the goal of speech. Instead there is an awakening into a world of the real, an awakening that takes place after the crumbling of the tower. We begin to hear another silence, the silence that follows its destruction: "and before I wake up/ the mess of my burnt bricks crumbles/ and turns back/ to clay" (14). The poem juxtaposes the awakening of the impulse to speak against the awakening into which the defeated impulse subsides. It juxtaposes, in other words, two sets of possible silences against one another: those associated with the impulse to speak, to integrate, to transcend, and those associated with a silence in history; those that arise within a poetics of representability, and those that occur with the breakdown of such a poetics altogether. The impulse that "is born from silence and seeks its conclusion in silence" (Dauenhauer) is overcome, as it were, by a different silence. Significantly, the second and final awakening takes place outside the literal borders of the poem, and, by extension, of language.

The reference to clay (chomer, in Hebrew), is a Biblical allusion to the clay or dust out of which God created Adam (17). The crumbling of the tower and the subsiding of the whisper, then, involve a return of man to clay, a reversal of creation, a decomposing of form. We are left with the silence of a void that is outside the range of hearing because it is outside human and created structures of thought, perception, and language, a silence of that which is, finally, not amenable to human symbolic manipulation.

This last awakening is an awakening to a knowledge that is excluded from the poem. The story of the "speechless whisper" is the story of the nature and conditions of that knowledge: its unrepresentability within language. For all of its traditional use of narrative and image, Pagis's poem does not claim a mimetic relationship to its subject. It relies instead on the fact that we listen to stories armed with basic human understandings upon which storytelling is built, and which, in this case, the reader uses to infer what has been omitted from the narrative. It is on the basis of this familiarity—of a shared knowledge of the ways in which we experience the world and articulate that traumatic knowledge—that the reader is able to construct some sense of the conditions that lead to a breakdown of language.

The Silence of the Throat

Giselle Brelet clarifies the role of the self or mind in the motion toward silence that is signified by Pagis's "migdal" or tower:

> Be it possession or expectation,—endowed with whatever affective quality, silence must invoke what goes beyond it, the transcending act of the mind. It is filled by the mind, for it is the mind's own presence to itself.[22]

The tower image implicates a silence of symbolic integration at the very same time that the play of whisper and wind in the containing structure of the tower suggests the human throat in which the voice and its structures of articulation reside. The physiological metaphor inscribes a human physicality into the poem. That bodily presence is at its densest in the concluding images of the poem in which the tower—as the "mess of my burnt bricks"—is a figure for the desymbolized (read, without speech) state of self into which the poem resolves.

The complex and layered sensibility of the poem involves an uneasy coupling of symbol and flesh, of a silence associated with metaphysical longing and with a very different silence, one that is rife with the lived experience of massive destruction in history. In another poem, "Brothers," Pagis writes:

> Cain is dumbstruck. His large hand
> gropes in the slaughtered throat in front of
> him:
> where has this silence burst from?   (5)

Silence in these lines is a bodily silence, a silence of the throat. In the figure of the tower in the first poem and here in the concreteness of reference to a "slaughtered throat," the silence projected embodies within it the materiality of the destruction to which it is a witness. It is a silence that disturbs because it is so freighted with bodies and with history and because it so easily reduces that other silence, the ardent and complex will to transcendence, to irrelevance.

Aharon Appelfeld describes his conflictedness and the tension of these two silences as they affect his own voice:

> If we had been able to shut up in an inner silence, that would have been right for us, but that was just a wish. We never actually stopped trying to say something, even in moments of greatest torpor. But all we succeeded to emit was a stutter, or worse, familiar, traditional words and fabrication. Afterwards we understood that nothing would be said unless new words and a new melody were found.[23]

Appelfeld speaks here of both a desire to remain silent and an impulse to speak, of stuttering and of music, of old words and of the need for new ones. "There are still songs to sing beyond mankind," the German poet Paul Celan writes.[24] The Yiddish poet and survivor of the Vilna ghetto, Abraham Sutzkever, similarly employs a familiar vocabulary of transcendence in a poetry attuned to the silence of historical destruction:

> . . . slaughtering silence weeps
> I hang—a shattered chord
> and dedicate my song to you.[25]

Sutzkever, like Pagis, uses the metaphor of a broken vocal/instrumental chord to suggest the problematic of articulation that lies at the heart of "historical horror." All of these writers acknowledge a familiar motive of transcendence, the need for words that will move through time, like music, to "the word beyond speech," at the same time that they point to the dilemma of voice for the writer who would hear the "slaughtering silence" of historical destruction.

In his discussion of the poet Paul Celan, Alvin Rosenfeld touches upon differences in the kinds of silences with which we are here concerned. We cannot, he says, write of the silence or

> speechlessness of an existential angst, for with Celan we are well beyond that. The night of Holderlin and even of Nietzsche was precipitated by that radical transvaluation of values that abandoned each of them to extreme states of ontological loneliness and terror, finally trapping the poet and philosopher in madness. The night that Celan knew was darker and more terrible still, for this time history determined it literally, not metaphorically and swept away innocent millions including the poet's own family into empty spaces in the sky.[26]

In another poem, "Footprints," Pagis refers to the silences with which he is concerned as a new language to be studied. Its parts of speech describe a set of relations that are the deep structure, the "heavenly grammar," of the universe, not as mind would construct it but as history and silence in history would reveal it. The poet, in Stephen Mitchell's beautiful translation from the Hebrew, must learn "the declensions and ascensions" of this very different silence:

> Where to begin?
> I don't even know how to ask.
> Too many tongues are mixed in my mouth. But
> at the crossing of these winds,
> very diligent, I immerse myself
> in the laws of heavenly grammar: I am learning
> the declensions and ascensions of
> silence.   (33)

Writing in this other language, speech takes different forms. Pagis writes, not about the impossibility of ascent to vision but of the difficulty of descent to the experience he would represent:

> Frozen and burst, clotted,
> scarred,
> charred, choked.
>
> If it has been ordained that I pull out of
>   here,
> I'll try to descend rung by rung,
> I hold on to each one carefully—
> but there is no end to the ladder, and already
> no time. All I can still do is fall
> into the world.   (33)

And like Appelfeld, Celan, and Sutzkever, he writes of a conflictedness of voice, the impulse that, after each collapse of the tower, searches the silence again for "that which opens the way for language's potency . . . ," that cannot forget the old impulses, the old grammar and poetics:

> And my throat says to me:
> If you are still alive, give me an opening, I
> must praise.   (34)

Voice and Silence

In both the Pagis poem and the film *Shoah*, voice is a key to the voicing of a silence in history. Barthes, in his essay, "The Grain of the Voice," asks, "isn't the entire space of the voice an infinite one?"[27] And he continues, "the grain is the body in the voice as it sings, the hand as it writes, the limb as it performs." Barthes is writing quite literally of the human speaking and singing voice. The point of the essay is to question a formal aesthetics, one that does not hear in the voice a living, human body

in living relationship to itself and its experience.[28] Simone de
Beauvoir also focuses on the physical manifestation of voice in
her discussion of *Shoah*:

> Voices: During most of the film all the voices tell of
> the same things: the trains that arrived, the wagons
> being opened and corpses tumbling out, the thirst, the
> unawareness riddled with fear, the stripping and "disin-
> fection" procedures, the gas chambers being opened. But
> never does it seem repetitive.

She describes the different voices, the points at which emotion
takes over the voice, the poise of the voice: that of Franz
Schomet, the SS Unterscharfuhrer at Treblinka, that of a train
driver who delivered Jewish children to concentration camp, of
a Sobibor station master, of peasants who lived just outside the
different camps, of survivors:

> And then there are the voices of the very rare Jewish sur-
> vivors of the camps. Two or three have managed to mas-
> ter a seeming serenity. But many can hardly speak—their
> voices break down and they burst into tears.   (iv)

De Beauvoir tells us that, although the stories of the survivors
are repetitive, we are not bored by them. She understands intuitively that the point is not the story told but the voice in which it
is told. She knows that an experience can be communicated only
through another experience; that only as we experience the voice
addressing us, the pauses and hesitations that mark it and flow
from experience, can we begin to understand. The stories of the
survivors in the film do not bore the viewer because the real story,
as in Pagis's "The Tower," is the story of the voice. As the voice
flows out of the body and into the world, out of experience and
toward a reconciliation with that experience, qualities of that flow
actively structure the silences that we hear.[29] The breakdown of
voice we witness in *Shoah* and the story of the voice that Pagis
recounts in his poem involve a specific gesture or human
response to the experience of historical catastrophe.[30]

In a comment on the poetry of First World War poet Wilfred Owen, Stephen Spender discusses the delicate issue of poetic voice in relation to the experience of catastrophe. Owen's poetry, he writes,

> . . . retains its Keatsian richness, but his subject matter mocks Keats' belief in a sensuous world of the imagination. The literal imagery of war parodies the richness of Romantic imagery. . . . The real agony turns on the poetic agonizing and strangles it with bare hands.[31]

Carolyn Forché, at the 1989 meeting of the International Association of Philosophy and Literature (IAPL), also addressed the question of poetic voice in the representation of historical catastrophe. Her talk was about a work then in progress and since published, *The Angel of History*, a book-length poem that takes the Holocaust and calamities of our century as its subject.[32] Forché stated that, as she began the work, her voice as a lyric poet immediately became problematic. The romantic tower of self and of language could not sustain her subject. She began to hear the voices of others, voices of people she had met. She described some of those encounters, especially one with a woman survivor who was briefly her hospital roommate. And she perceived the space of her voice as one in which others might articulate themselves. She directed her efforts to listening, not to the voice within herself, but to the voices of others not herself; not to a silence within, but to a world of history peopled with the bodies of those not here, to the voices of those who have been destroyed, hunted, dislocated, maimed, starved, and tortured.

Forché's historical material forced her to abandon her own poetic voice in a manner that closely parallels the crumbling of the tower/throat of Pagis's poem. In another poem, *Holocaust* by the objectivist poet Charles Reznikoff, the poet chooses to efface his voice entirely.[33] The poem is constructed as a collage of the voices of others, out of bits and pieces of testimony given at the Nuremberg trial. Charlotte Delbo's trilogy, *Auschwitz and After*, about her experiences in Auschwitz and in the numbed aftermath of her time there, is written in the highly untraditional and highly effective first-person-plural stream of consciousness.[34] The collective, historical "we" that includes herself and her comrades is a "we" of testimony and witnessing. By virtue of a stream-of-consciousness technique, it is also a "we" that locates itself within an experience. Both Reznikoff and Delbo privilege a voice that is branded by history in the effort to voice a silence within history.

Schwarz-Bart: Trauma and the Breakdown of Voice

The breakdown of voice described in the Pagis poem involves the breakdown of a poetic process, more fundamentally, of a speech process. The rupture of language, to which so many writers, critics, and philosophers refer in connection to the Holocaust, refers to this breakdown. The formally significant point to be made about imaginative representations of historical horror is that they characteristically place such a process at risk. Traditional images of transcendence accompany and ironically set up the implications of such a collapse: hence the collapse of the tower in the Pagis poem, of a music festival in *Badenheim 1939*, the use of bird imagery in this novel and in Jerzi Kosinski's *The Painted Bird*, and the imagery of song and of music in Celan and in Sutzkever. In each case, such an imagery accompanies a simple, rhetorical statement about a breakdown of speech in the face of historical catastrophe. ". . . it is especially important," Susan Shapiro writes, "to consider the testimony of this negative poesis for it witnesses to the shattering of the coherence and the negation of the meaningfulness of language itself."[35]

If we move from film and poetry to fiction in Holocaust literature, we find the story in Pagis's "The Tower" of a breakdown of voice, told and retold. André Schwarz-Bart's novel, *The Last of the Just*, is a beautifully written history of one family whose last descendant, Ernie Levy, dies at Auschwitz.[36] The title of the novel refers to an ancient Jewish legend according to which the continued existence of the world depends upon the existence of thirty-six hidden, righteous men. Ernie is the last of these. The novel follows Ernie from childhood to adulthood. The story of his assault (chapter 5 of section 5) by teacher and classmates ends with a breakdown of voice that is remarkable for its similarities to the story of Pagis's tower, at the same time that it portrays the human and psychic meaning of that breakdown in moving detail. Ernie and three other Jewish children have been humiliated in a variety of ways in the classroom by Herr Geek, a party ideologue who has replaced Herr Kremer. Assaulted physically and sexually by classmates after school and betrayed by his sweetheart, Ilse, Ernie closes his eyes:

> His eyes closed, the little boy imagined that the sweat, the saliva, the tears and the phlegm in which he was bathing were simply one and the same substance, welling up from some spring deep within his being, splitting its envelope now and flowing in the sunlight. All those liquids emanated from his own interior substance, blue-green, shadowy, viscous, not composed normally of flesh and bone, as he had once thought. . . .
> Time now seemed a bottomless sea.   (232)

Ernie fends off his attackers with his teeth. Alone, he makes his way home over a bridge and washes dried blood from a gash on his forehead. From this point forward to the end of the chapter, the narrative is not one of events but of their integration. The setting is pastoral and filled with detailed attention to childhood, to children's ways of thinking, feeling, and playing. Schwarz-Bart's portrait of a process that will culminate in the child's loss of voice begins with a moment of silence. Imagery of earth, of silence, of sky, and of play with insects suggest a depth of inner sifting through experience:

> The earth around him gave off its odors. All things were fixed, enveloped in the smells of the earth. The silence had that smell, and the exhalations of the sun, and the immutable blue of the sky. . . . With infinite gentleness, Ernie Levy set the ladybug on the end of his vertical thumb. . . .   (239)

The silence ends as Ernie cracks the ladybug between his fingers and rolls it into a pulp. The meadow then fills with sound as Ernie seeks out one insect victim after another:

> ... setting this atom of matter in the hollow of his hand, he rubbed it between his palms at great length until the ladybug was annihilated, leaving only a grayish stain.
> Then raising his head, he realized that the silence had just died.
> The meadow was alive with the rustling of wings, with the movement of grass, with that invisible, heavy quivering of life. The earth itself was seething defiantly.
> (240)

Sound is associated here with wings, grass, life forces, defiance. But the insect murders that follow finally wear Ernie out:

> Each insect death cost him more. Each death added its cortege of soft ordure, and now they were filling his stomach—viscid liquors on his palms but dismembered insects, seething and suffering, in his own belly. . . .
> Ernie raised his eyelids and drowned in the fallen sky.
> (241, 42)

The necessary and intact world of childhood cannot put itself back together. The child views birds flying above, perceives himself in contrast to be an insect, and cries out repeatedly, "I was nothing," as he buries his head in the ground for half an hour. Surprisingly, his eyes are without tears:

> He seemed to be hailing someone far off, a being buried deep in the earth from whom he wanted only an echo. But his cries only exaggerated the silence, and the vermin remained lively in his belly. His mouth was full of grass and dirt. Finally he knew that nothing would answer his call, for that call was born of nothing: God could not hear it. It was precisely here that Ernie Levy, the little boy, felt burdened by his body and decided to let that burden fall.   (242)

There is a cleavage that occurs inside Ernie. With the assault upon his physical integrity, something breaks inside the child and as a consequence of that break, his speech loses its substance, his call is "born of nothing"; he is nothing and God cannot hear his cry. Domains of experience and of language have fallen out of communication with one another. Just as the tower crumbled in the Pagis poem, selfhood here shrivels to nothing in the silence so that "his cries only exaggerated the silence."[37] As with Améry, it is social assault in an historical world that forecloses speech for Ernie.

Schwarz-Bart underlines the interruption of a living relationship of the self to the world from which it draws sustenance in language suggestive of an infant at the breast:

> As he thought, "I was nothing," the little boy buried his face against the earth and intoned his first cries. At the same instant he felt astonishment that his eyes should be empty of tears. For half an hour he cried out, his mouth against the earth.   (242)

Once the umbilicus joining self and world is cut, Ernie experiences the silence of stillborn speech, a silence described as a foreclosure of relationship between the self and God: "Finally he knew that nothing would answer his call, for that call was born of nothing, God could not hear it." At the crucial level, then, of speaking, of an open transaction between language and experience, silence produced by traumatic experience does not bring speech into being, but overwhelms it. Schwarz-Bart thus portrays, in the simplest possible human terms, a rupture in speech that one philosopher calls "the Shoah-rupturing of God-language and of the very foundations of speech and writing."[38]

As in the Pagis poem, there is a sense of rising energy that precedes collapse. The same sequence of a silence followed by a gathering of energy and its collapse plays itself out in the final pages of the novel. The scene takes place years later. Ernie is an adult. He, his beloved Golda, and a group of children he has taken into his protection are standing in the gas chamber. Again, Schwarz-Bart notes the silence:

When the layers of gas had covered everything, there
was silence in the dark sky of the room for perhaps a
minute. . . .

The silence does not last. It gives way to a rising energy, not of
grass, birds and earth, but of words:

And first a stream, then a cascade, an irrepressible, majestic torrent, the poem that through the smoke of fires and
above the funeral pyres of history . . . the old love poem
that they traced in letters of blood on the earth's hard
crust unfurled in the gas chamber, enveloped it, van-
quished its somber, abysmal snickering: "SHEMA YIS-
RAEL ADONAI ELOHENU ADONAOI EH'OTH. . . ."
                                                                    (373)

The energy and protest of life forces within the gas chambers
fills the silence with words that form "a stream, then a cascade,
an irrepressible, majestic torrent, the poem. . . ." We are back to
Broch and his sense of language as a flow toward "the word
beyond speech." The words of the poem fill the gas chamber
and momentarily vanquish it until:

The voices died one by one in the course of the unfin-
ished poem. The dying children had already dug their
nails into Ernie's thighs. . . .   (373)

Within half an hour Ernie's body is found by the Son-
derkommando and burnt with millions of others in the crema-
tory ovens. So much for life forces, for language, for transcendence. But reminders of transcendence are not so easily laid to
rest. The closing page of the novel continues to juxtapose
imagery of transcendence against more chilling references to
massive death in the disturbing manner of Pagis's tower image.
The dark organic particles of smoke that soon fill the sky rise
upward at the same time that they are heavy with the organic
matter of destroyed life:

For the smoke that rises from crematoriums obeys physical laws like any other: the particles come together and
disperse according to the wind that propels them. (374)

Turning his words to the reader, Schwarz-Bart offers a prayer in
which words of praise to the Creator alternate with names of
death camps. "And praised. **Auschwitz**. Be. **Maidanek**. . . ." The
language of praise, of prayer and of God provides a final affirmation of human value even as it articulates the extinction of all
human value. The tension generated by this striking interpola-
tion is one of bald oppositions. The ritual and rhythmic formulation of that opposition is connected to the drive for vitality,
meaning, and affirmation that is rudely negated in the naming
of the death camps. The prayer is jarring and disturbing in ways
that so much imagery in this literature disturbs; it is as though
the world we knit together so arduously with each of our words
is simultaneously and frantically unknit.

Kosinski: The Premise of Trust in Language

In a poem entitled "Draft of a Reparations Agreement,"
Pagis makes ironic reference to the loss of voice with which his
poetry is so centrally concerned:

> All right, gentlemen who cry blue murder as
> always,
> nagging miracle-makers,
> quiet!
> Everything will be returned to its place,
> paragraph after paragraph.
> The scream back into the throat.   (27)

Jerzy Kosinski's *The Painted Bird* is about a scream ripped
out of the throat of the child protagonist and narrator of his
novel.[39] The narrative and dramatic structure of the novel turn
on this loss of voice and its recovery. In his introduction,
Kosinski points out that a million people were killed in his

native Poland as a result of direct military action during the war, while five and one half million were exterminated. And it is the physical possibility of speech that is thereby placed in jeopardy.[40]

The protagonist and child narrator of *The Painted Bird* spends the war years wandering from village to village exchanging his menial services for food and a roof over his head. At one point he is asked to carry the missal during a church service. The episode culminates a series of atrocities suffered, witnessed, and in one case, precipitated by the child to save his life. In one such scene, the child is repeatedly hung by straps from a ceiling by his "protector" Garbos, who leaves his vicious dog to watch the child for signs of tiring.

At the service, the child, slight in build, slips with the missal. The peasants grab him in fury and take him outside. The child tries to beg for mercy but no sound comes out of his throat. Realizing that the peasants intend to throw him into a large manure pit, he tries to shout again without success. Thrown into the pit, he miraculously climbs out despite the undertow and realizes what has occurred:

> Suddenly I realized that something had happened to my voice. I tried to cry out, but my tongue flapped helplessly in my mouth. I had no voice. I was terrified. . . .
>
> I sat down. The last cry that I had uttered under the falling missal still echoed in my ears, was it the last cry I would ever utter? Was my voice escaping with it like a solitary duck call straying over a huge pond?   (140)

Voice is no longer located in the child's body. Being and the power of articulating being have been physically separated. With this severing of the connection between language and experience, the opaqueness of history, its silence, and its resistance to speech are inscribed into the novel and into the body of the child until the child's recovery of speech in the very last lines. As in the Schwarz-Bart novel, the breakdown of speech is the manifestation of a larger event and loss within the self, an

event that results in muteness. The child marks his disposses-
sion of his voice by figuring it as something separate from himself and from his body: a bird.

> Where was it now? I could envision my voice flying
> alone under the highly-arched, vaulting ribs of the
> church roof. I saw it knocking against the cold walls, the
> holy pictures, against the thick panes of colored glass in
> the windows, which the sun's rays could scarcely pene-
> trate. I followed its aimless wanderings through the dark
> aisles, where it wafted from the alter to the pulpit, from
> pulpit to balcony, from the balcony to the altar again, dri-
> ven by the multichorded sound of the organ and the
> groundswell of the singing crowd.   (140, 41)

Voice is seen here as a moving bird that cannot freely ascend
to the sky but is trapped in the dark spaces of the church, much
like the "small speechless whisper" that is similarly trapped in
the "twisted corridor" of Pagis's tower. The bird image in this
passage, with its emphasis upon motion, suggests language as it
dwells and moves through silence and in time. The child's
muteness is the physical mark by which traumatic experience
interrupts that flight and drains the self of the vital connectedness to itself and to its experience that is the condition of speech.

The separation of body and voice follows a scene of torture
and takes place in a setting that is both religious and communal.
A breakdown within the human family that turns against its
own most vulnerable members thus leads directly to the child's
loss of speech. Jean Améry comments on the experience of torture:

> . . . with the very first blow that descends on him he loses
> something we will perhaps temporarily call "trust in the
> world. . . . the certainty that the other person will . . .
> respect my physical, and with it also my metaphysical,
> being. The boundaries of my body are also the bound-
> aries of my self. My skin surface shields me against the
> external world. . . .

> At the first blow, however, this trust in the world
> breaks down. . . . If no help can be expected, this physi-
> cal overwhelming by the other then becomes an existen-
> tial consummation of destruction altogether.   (28)

The historical assault depicted in Kosinski's novel thus breaks
down a primary relationship of trust that bonds the self to the
world. Voice is premised on that trust and depends upon a connection to the world that is radically undermined by historical
trauma.

Borowski: Birthing the Word, a Process and Its Burdens

Tadeusz Borowski, a Pole who was interned in Auschwitz as
a political prisoner and who took his life in Warsaw in 1951 at
the age of twenty-nine, is well known for a collection of short
stories entitled *This Way for the Gas, Ladies and Gentlemen*.[41] The
stories, which record Borowski's experiences in Auschwitz and
in post-war Germany, logically progress to the final story, "The
World of Stone," which is an account of the struggle to articulate
the writer's experience of the world. The sequence leads from a
series of stories about the concentration camp experience to a
story whose focus is language and the repeated falterings of
words that cannot describe that experience.

"World of Stone" is about a succession of images that assault
the narrator as he makes his way through a crowd to accomplish
an errand. If, on one level, "World of Stone" takes place after the
war and follows the other stories chronologically, it seems at the
same time to move backward to the outset of each story, to reca-
pitulate the burden of each narrative, the difficulty of its articulation. The assault on the individual in the concentration camps
that is the setting and action of almost all of the preceding stories is a prelude to this very story and its burden.

"World of Stone," then, is about the silence that overcomes
voice as a result of the sustained assault described in story after
story. It is a detailed examination of "the exchange between
experience and language." The image, unlike the tower of

Pagis's poem, collapses not once, but four times. The repetition is a measure of Borowski's struggle with his experience of the historical world in its overwhelming presence.

The story, we are told, in the opening lines, is about gestation, the gestation of this very knowledge. As in the Pagis poem, there is an impulse that searches for the words with which to voice the experience, and there is a silence located in trauma that resists the articulation:

> For quite some time now, like the foetus inside a womb, a terrible knowledge had been ripening within me, and filling my soul with frightened foreboding that the Infinite Universe is inflating at incredible speed, like some ridiculous soap bubble.   (177)

As this knowledge ripens, the writer goes on an errand through one of the poorest districts of the city. Repeatedly as he walks, the sights, smells, sounds, and activities around him, and especially, the physical details of the people around him, cluster and form an image: the image formed, however, falls apart. The impulse to give form does not find an inner space or silence out of which the flow of language may shape itself, but stumbles upon its own umbilicus:

> Sometimes it seems to me that even my physical sensibilities have coagulated and stiffened within me like resin. In contrast to years gone by, when I observed the world with wide-open, astonished eyes, and walked along every street alert, like a young man on a parapet, I can now push through the liveliest crowd with indifference and rub against hot female bodies without the slightest emotion, even though the girls may try to seduce me with the bareness of their knees and their coiled intricately coiffed hair.   (178)

The problem is precisely the breakdown of the underlying and animating erotic bonding of the narrator to the world, a bonding that is the premise of symbol-making and a condition of speech.

Desire does not fail before an image or vision receding before it but is itself victim to the lethargy and inner numbness of traumatic experience. Like the muteness of the child in Kosinski's novel, this numbing becomes the condition of the self in the world:

> At this point I must confess that although since the end of the war I very rarely force myself to polish my shoes and almost never shake the mud off my trouser turn-ups, that although it is a great effort for me to shave my face, chin and neck twice weekly, and although I bite off my fingernails in order to save time, and never hunt after some books or materials, thus relating the deliberate senselessness of my own fate to that of the Universe, I have recently begun to leave my house on hot summer afternoons to go for long, lonely strolls through the poorest districts of my city.   (177, 78)

The world cannot seduce him into speech. The vigor and directness of the description carry desire for what Maurice Merleau-Ponty calls "sonorous speech about the world" into the texture of the reading experience:

> And I can see as distinctly as if I were looking in a mirror, the ruins, already overgrown with fresh, green grass, the peasant women, with their flour-thickened sour cream and their rancid-smelling dresses, the trolley-bus rails, the rag-ball and the children, the workers with their muscular arms and tired eyes, the street, the square and the angry babbler rising above it into the restless clouds blown on by a strong wind—I can see all this suddenly float into the air and then drop, all in a tangle right at my feet—like the broken reflection of trees and sky in a mountain stream rushing under a bridge.   (178)

Borowski's language, in this story, creates an energy, a pulse of successive and graphic images, that betrays the liveliness of the impulse that would seek out the word even as it speaks to us of trauma, silence, and resistance.

The narrator continues to wrestle with the impulse that "opens the way for language's potency" and with that in memory which interferes with the "exchange between experience and language." The next image of failed articulation implicates a perceived chaos of experience that finally "flows along the street, down the gutter, and seeps into space with a loud gurgle, like water into a sewer." The chaos is a chaos of the sensuous, visible present, a "gust of cosmic gale" that sweeps the bodies of men, women, and children on the street into an imagined whirlpool of their dismembered parts. Borowski describes the bodies with visual, sensual, and sexual detail that give this surreal image a crisp and horrifying materiality:

> Through half-open eyes I see with satisfaction that once again a gust of the cosmic gale has blown the crowd into the air, all the way up to the treetops, sucked the human bodies into a huge whirlpool, twisted their lips open in terror, mingled the children's rosy cheeks with the hairy chests of the men, entwined the clenched fists with strips of women's dresses, thrown snow-white thighs on the top, like foam, with hats and fragments of heads tangled in hair-like seaweed peeping from below.   (178, 79)

Once again, the image-making process breaks down as the sensuousness of language recalls a helplessness of living bodies only too graphically. The pressure of overdimensional experience, of "this gigantic stew," cannot flow into speech but slushes its way into a sewer.

Failure of the image brings new effort. The world, grasped in sensuous terms, continues to overwhelm the narrator; the image falters:

> I enter with a casual air, the modest but cozy little rooms occupied by people of importance and ask, perhaps a trifle too politely, for things that are perhaps too trivial, but to which nevertheless I am entitled—but which, of course, cannot keep the world from swelling and bursting like an over-ripe pomegranate, leaving behind but a handful of grey, dry ashes.   (179)

Desire to find the word that will give speech to the world tags the narrator like a devoted pet. The world in which the death camp is one possibility and this cozy office with its marble staircase another overwhelms the narrator with both longing and fear. The image of desired wholeness, the over-ripe pomegranate, swells and bursts into the parched ash of the real.

Finally, back in his room, with extraordinary effort, the writer takes out his utensils. Distant sounds of the street intrude upon the silence. Borowski notes those sounds one after the other as though the relation of the physical silence and noises that surround him were analogous to an inner silence that must sift through the noise of experience as it searches for the words to trace onto the empty page before him. In memory he recalls once again the physical details of the people and places he passed in the course of the day. The act of writing does not occur within the story or even in a future outside the story. This time we do not witness the failure or the success of an image to negotiate the "exchange between experience and language." We know only that the process is to begin yet again, that the narrator now seated at a table will "attempt to grasp the true significance of the events, things and people I have seen," that he intends to write about the world as he has experienced it, "this unchanging, difficult world chiselled out of stone" (180).

The Snow of That Left Unspoken

If we briefly return to the poem by Pagis, we now understand that the method of speaking about a silence outside language and the mind involves speaking about the desire to articulate. Traumatic utterance tells the story of that desire: its impediments, difficulties and resistances. But it also leaves something out. The experiences it would bring to us are never revealed except by inference in the same way that the drawing of a figure on a clean sheet of paper also gives shape to the spaces surrounding the figure, in which the figure resides, and in relation to which the figure exists. Unlike the silence of a postmodern sensibility, the silence of traumatic utterance is very specific in the relation of the self to words and to silence. Paul Celan's poem "With a Variable Key" is a description of those relations:

> With a variable key
> you unlock the house in which
> drifts the snow of that left unspoken.
> Always what key you choose
> depends on the blood that spurts
> from your eye, or your mouth or your ear.
>
> You vary the key, you vary the word
> That is free to drift with the flakes.
> What snowball will form around the word
> depends on the wind that rebuffs you.[42]

Here is not the silence of a world beyond language, nor the birthing silence in which the formal impulse presses for articulation, nor the symbolic depths of silence that follows closure. Instead, Celan brings us a silence that forms protectively, like a snowball, around the word, a silence that is at the same time at the mercy of unpredictable historical winds: "What snowball will form depends on the wind that rebuffs you." Unlike the snowman in Wallace Stevens's "Snowman," snow here is not alien but intimate.[43] It does not proceed from an otherness outside the self but is excreted, as it were, from within that very self. It is the "snow of that left unspoken."

Chapter 4

Historical Horror and the Literary Act of Witness:
An Examination of Elie Wiesel's *Night*

> Because even in direct experience everyday reality is nothing
> but codified abstraction. Only in rare moments of life do we
> truly stand face to face with the event and, with it, reality.
> —*Jean Améry*

In chapter 1 we saw that the attempt to represent horror
whose origins are outside the mind in history brings into play a
host of narrative and aesthetic strategies whose purpose is to
authenticate: to make real the unreal. "Today at this very
moment as I sit writing at a table, I am not convinced that these
things really happened," Primo Levi writes.[1] And reviewing her
manuscript, Charlotte Delbo, whose work we will examine in
some detail in the next chapter, is troubled. She does not question the reality of events, only the faithfulness of her account: "I
am no longer sure," she writes, "that what I have written is true,
but I am sure that it happened."[2]

If the one writer questions the facticity of events he lived
through in Auschwitz and the other questions the faithfulness of
her written account, also of her Auschwitz experience, both point

to the way that the experience of historical horror undermines the "exchange between language and experience." Extreme experience for Levi has outstripped his own capacity to integrate and claim a large and important segment of his life experience. What new verbal situation does this create? Was Levi in Auschwitz? What words will Levi find for an experience that cannot have occurred but did? Delbo, rereading her own work, questions the ability of her words to open the realm of extreme experience to us. Words cannot speak a truth to which they are not privy.

If the witness's claim to have personally experienced or observed a particular event liberates narrative from the constraints of verisimilitude, such a narrative, for all of its evidentiary claims, can be fraught with its own set of difficulties. Piotr Rawicz, in his novel *Blood from the Sky*, creates a narrative within which a conventional narrative mode falls apart and is replaced by eyewitness testimony that is then, also, revealed to be flawed.[3] The claim is not that the novel has revealed its subject to us, but that this subject must always escape telling in any form whatever. Rawicz's narrative brings into view the silent, untellable nature of historical horror and asks us to look, not only at the inadequacy of any narrative account of historical horror, but at the inadequacy of even eyewitness testimony. Literary texts that take historical horror for their subject inevitably reach for narrative and aesthetic strategies to navigate the treacherous spaces separating the realm of experience from the realm of language. Inevitably, such texts are caught up in the effort to bridge those realms by an act of literary witnessing.

In this chapter I explore a central text of literary witnessing, Elie Wiesel's *Night*.[4] *Night* addresses the issue of the unreal, not through a disavowal of narrative and of witnessing itself, but within a transaction of reader and writer. Rolf Krause discusses this transaction in his study of German autobiographical writing by concentration camp survivors, "Truth But Not Art."[5] Krause notes the way in which extreme experience separates the individual from others. He explains that:

the disturbance may . . . arise . . . in the communication process itself: if the partners do not speak the same language communication cannot be successful. It need not necessarily be because the partners do not want to understand one another but because they are not capable of doing so—their fields of experience and their present situations and needs are too divergent. . . .

The distance between reader and writer "cannot be bridged one-sidedly," he writes, "by way of confrontation with facts." Instead:

> . . . a confrontation with communication partners can only have genuine informational value within the framework of a self-instruction of the communication partners about the differences that stand in the way of successful communication. This however, requires adopting an attitude in writing which does not exhaust itself in the referential function of language, in the role of a repartee as a mediator of facts—rather the author must treat the writing process as a chance to achieve mutual understanding which means that he has to incorporate both his dialogue partner and himself into the communication process.[6]

The narrative of *Night* incorporates into itself the situation of the reader of such a literary work. Thus the topos of the rejected witness and the figure of Madame Schachter function as ways of narrativizing the resistances of the reader to the experience (Auschwitz) that Wiesel wishes to portray. The effect of Wiesel's strategy of narration is to make possible within narrative the reception of the concentration camp world in all of its violence and unmitigated facticity.[7]

Wiesel's method depends upon a series of repetitions in which what is at stake is a breakdown of critical illusions. The experience of the reader parallels Hans Robert Jauss's striking description of the way one comes to apprehend "the real." "For progress . . . in the experience of life, the most important moment is the 'disappointment of expectations.'" He quotes Karl Popper:

It resembles the experience of a blind person who runs into an obstacle and thereby experiences its existence. Through the falsification of our assumptions we actually make contact with 'reality.' The refutation of our errors is the positive experience we gain from reality.[8]

Eliezer's tale is the story of a series of shattered expectations, his and our own. The repetition of this "disappointment," of optimism proven hollow and warnings rejected, is the crucial aesthetic fact or condition within which the reader then experiences Wiesel's account of Auschwitz, of Buna, of Gleiwitz, and of Buchenwald.

Night opens with Eliezer's search for a teacher of mystical knowledge. He finds that teacher in Moshe the Beadle:

And Moshe the Beadle, the poor barefoot of Sighet, talked to me for long hours of the revelations and mysteries of the cabbala. It was with him that my initiation began. We would read together, ten times over, the same page of the Zohar. Not to learn it by heart, but to extract the divine essence from it. (17)

Only a paragraph later, Moshe is deported. He is shot but escapes from a mass grave in one of the Galician forests of Poland near Kolomaye and returns to Sighet in order to warn the Jews there. He describes children used as targets for machine guns and the fate of a neighbor, Malka, and of Tobias the tailor.

Moshe is not believed, not even by his disciple, Eliezer. The Jews of Sighet resist the news that Moshe has brought them. The first two chapters of *Night* circle around this question of resistance to the factuality of historical horror:

"I wanted to come back to Sighet to tell you the story of my death. . . . And see how it is, no one will listen to me. . . ." (16)

And we, the Jews of Sighet were waiting for better days, which would not be long in coming now.

Yes, we even doubted that he (Hitler) wanted to exterminate us.

Was he going to wipe out a whole people? Could he exterminate a population scattered throughout so many countries? So many millions! What methods could he use? And in the middle of the twentieth century?   (17)

Wiesel describes the optimism that reasserts itself after the shock of the arrival of German troops in Sighet. Sighet is divided into a big and little ghetto. ". . . little by little life returned to normal. The barbed wire which fenced us in did not cause us any real fear" (21).

The intensity of the resistance peaks in the boxcar in which Eliezer and his family are taken to the death camp. Madame Shachter, distraught by the separation from her pious husband and two older sons, has visions of fire: "Jews, listen to me! I can see a fire! There are huge flames! It is a furnace!" (35). Her words prey on nerves, fan fears, dispel illusion: ". . . we felt that an abyss was about to open beneath our bodies." She is gagged and beaten by her fellow Jews and neighbors. Even as her cries are silenced, the chimneys of Auschwitz come into view:

We had forgotten the existence of Madame Shachter. Suddenly we heard terrible screams:
"Jews, look! Look through the window! Flames! Look!"
And as the train stopped, we saw this time that flames were gushing out of a tall chimney into the black sky.   (38)

Eliezer's failure to believe the witness and the community's failure to hear the words of the truthful prophetess prepare the reader for Eliezer's story by first examining the defenses that Eliezer, the community, and, implicitly, the reader, bring to historical realities too threatening to credit or even to imagine. Only at this point does Wiesel bring his narrative inside the gates of Auschwitz.[9]

It is this moment and its imaginative reception with which Wiesel is concerned. The murder of Mme. Schacter within sight of the chimneys of Auschwitz makes similar denial on the part of the reader impossible. The reader has been stripped of his or her defenses in advance of Eliezer's arrival at Auschwitz. Wiesel's carefully wrought narrative of resistance, defense, and denial of the historical catastrophe overtaking the Jewish community in Sighet moves the reader from a fortified position to an open undefended one vis-à-vis the impact of the narrative from this point forward in the narrative.

The use and subversion of the traditional quest story defines the stakes of the narrative from the first page of *Night*. Eliezer is devoted to his studies of Talmud. His decision to study Kabbalah with Moshe focuses the narrative on the problematic of reality and imbues it with the spiritual longings of a mystical quest:

> "There are a thousand and one gates leading into the orchard of mystical truth. Every human being has his own gate. . . .
>
> And throughout those evenings a conviction grew in me that Moshe the Beadle would draw me with him into eternity, into that time where question and answer would become one.   (14)

Night begins with Eliezer's search for a teacher of mystical knowledge and ends with Eliezer's contemplating his image in a mirror after his liberation from Buchenwald. The book thus proposes a search for ultimate knowledge in terms that are traditional, while the knowledge it offers is historical, radical, and subversive. Knowing, in the quasi-religious framework in which Wiesel has located his story, is no mere knowing. The final and most violent shattering of human expectations occurs as Eliezer, newly arrived in Auschwitz, sees a truck filled with children who are dumped into a fiery ditch. Eliezer cannot believe what he has seen:

> I pinched my face. Was I still alive? Was I awake? I could not believe it. How could it be possible for them to burn people, children, and for the world to keep silent? No, none of this could be true. It was a nightmare. . . .
>
>   (42)

The language of horrific fact registers the crumbling of a potential world of forms and of expression before certain kinds of facts, certain kinds of experiences. Eliezer's words mark that crumbling. He addresses his disbelief as words retreat from the fact and illuminate, instead, the obscure and vast terrain of human resistance: a resistance of the body ("I pinched my face. Was I alive?") as well as of the mind ("Was I awake. . . . It was a nightmare").[10] The sight of the children thrown into burning pits is followed by an interruption of the narrative in which the first-person narrator addresses the reader directly and swears never to forget what he has witnessed.

In *The Differend: Phrases in Dispute*, Jean-François Lyotard is concerned with exactly such intransigent material of experience and the onus it places on language. He explains what he means by a "differend:"

> The *differend* is the unstable state and instant of language in which something which ought to be able to be phrased cannot yet be phrased. This state involves silence which is a negative sentence, but it also appeals to sentences possible in principle. What is ordinarily called sentiment signals this fact. "You can't find the words to say it," and so on. A great deal of searching is necessary to find new rules of formation and linkage of sentences capable of expressing the *differend* betrayed by sentiment. . . . It is the stake of a literature, a philosophy, perhaps a politics, to bear witness to *differends* by finding idioms for them.[11]

The "literary act of witnessing," and Wiesel's *Night* in particular, locate themselves in precisely such an instant.[12] It is an instant that marks the wrenching apart of a world of words from a world of experience, that brings the world of language and the world outside language—worlds that under usual conditions of representing are open to one another and dialogic—into the uncomfortable position of two adjacent keys on a piano when simultaneously pressed and held. The sounds they produce jar the ear.

Night brings us the collision of those two worlds. The dual motifs of spiritual quest and violent disillusion of a deeply religious young man bring the opacity and separateness of those structures—structures of mind, desire, and language and structures of experience and world—into violent juxtaposition. The confrontation with facts of utter horror opens up an abyss created in the wake of horrific fact. The opening up in Wiesel's *Night* occurs in the intertwining of two stories, the first a story about words, and the second a story about experience.

After witnessing living children thrown into flames, Eliezer and his father conclude that this is to be Eliezer's fate as well. Eliezer decides to avoid such a slow agony by running to a nearby electrified fence and electrocuting himself. Wiesel proceeds to tell us the story of that decision and of its reversal. The story of the attempted suicide is intertwined with another, the story of the Kaddish. The narrative thus literally sets the two stories, the two worlds—one that includes the witnessed horror of the deliberate burning alive of children, and one of words, forms, faith and God—reverberating against one another.

Hearing his fellow Jews murmur the Kaddish, a formula of praise of the Almighty that is the traditional prayer for the dead, Eliezer first revolts:

> For the first time, I felt revolt rise up in me. Why should I bless His name? The Eternal Lord of the Universe, the All-Powerful and Terrible, was silent. What had I to thank Him for?   (43)

The Jews continue their march and Eliezer begins to count the steps before he will jump at the wire.

> Ten steps still. Eight. Seven. We marched slowly on, as though following a hearse at our own funeral. . . . There it was now, right in front of us, the pit and its flames. I gathered all that was left of my strength, so that I could break from the ranks and throw myself upon the barbed wire. In the depths of my heart, I bade farewell to my father, to the whole universe. . . .   (44)

Even as Eliezer bids farewell to his father and the universe, an unanticipated event takes place:

> . . . and, in spite of myself, the words formed themselves and issued in a whisper from my lips: *Yitgadal veyitkadach shmé raba.* . . . May His name be blessed and magnified. . . . My head was bursting. The moment had come. I was face to face with the Angel of Death. . . .   (44)

Eliezer does not run to the wire. The entire group turns left and enters a barracks. The narrator, when he sees what he sees, revolts—but briefly. When faced with the horror of an electrocuted death, the holy words rise unbidden to his lips. The worlds of experience and of language could not, at this moment, be further apart. Experience is entirely beyond words. Words are utterly inadequate to experience.

The Kaddish is itself a form of testimony, the testimony and ritual affirmation of a congregation of believers to God's Oneness. The narrative of reversal, of Eliezer's decision not to run to the wire, turns on the appositioning of competing testimonies: the testimony of the eyes and history and the testimony of words; the testimony of events and that of the entire spiritual and linguistic vocabulary to which Eliezer's life had been so committed. The scene closes with Eliezer pressing his father's hand. His father responds with a question: "Do you remember Madame Schachter, in the train?"

The words of the Kaddish are transformed by the context in which they are recited. As the Jews look at the flames they assume will soon consume them and utter the words of the Kaddish, the words do not affirm God and His existence so much as they voice the disjunctions of a world of experience and one of faith. They point directly to that which "ought to be able to be phrased" but "cannot yet be phrased" and hence include the "silence which is a negative sentence" (Lyotard). The very revising of the meanings that are contained by the words of the Kaddish is a literary attempt "to find new rules of formation and linkage of sentences capable of expressing the *differend.*" The oath of witnessing that directly follows the narration of extremity is particularly fascinating for the "rules of formation and linkage of sentences" with which it responds to historical horror.

The passage, the most famous in Wiesel's oeuvre, is a tour de force of contradiction and of formal dissonances that are not reconciled, but juxtaposed and held up for inspection. Paradoxically, Wiesel's oath, like *Night* itself, constructs itself out of the very language that it renounces; his testimony against God and faith is fashioned in a grammar, out of sentences, and in the powerful grip of that faith:

> Never shall I forget that night, the first night in camp, which has turned my life into one long night, seven times cursed and seven times sealed.   (44)

Eliezer's words take the form of an oath never to forget this night of his arrival. The oath, the recourse to metaphorical language ("which has turned my life into one long night"), the reference to curses and phraseology ("seven times cursed . . .") echo the Biblical language in which Eliezer was so steeped. He continues:

> Never shall I forget that smoke. Never shall I forget the little faces of the children, whose bodies I saw turned into wreaths of smoke beneath a silent blue sky.   (44)

The oath is one of protest, the "silent blue sky," an accusation:

> Never shall I forget those flames which consumed my faith forever.

Here and in the sentences that follow, Wiesel uses the rhythms, verbal energy, imagery, and conventions of the Bible to challenge, accuse, and deny God:

> Never shall I forget that nocturnal silence which deprived me, for all eternity, of the desire to live. Never shall I forget those moments which murdered my God and my soul and turned my dreams to dust. Never shall I forget these things, even if I am condemned to live as long as God Himself. Never.   (44)

The elaborate oath of remembrance recalls the stern Biblical admonitions of remembrance. The negative formulation of the oath and the incremental repetition of the word "never" register defiance and anger even as the same eight repetitions of "never" circumscribing the passage give it rhythmic structure and ceremonial shape.

The passage uses the poetry and language of faith to attest a shattering of faith. In a sparely written, tightly constructed narrative it is the only extended poetic moment. It is a climactic moment and, strangely, in a work that so powerfully undercuts the pinions of words and language, a rhetorical moment: a moment constructed out of words and the special effects and properties of their combinations, a moment that hovers above the abyss of human extremity in uncertain relationship to it.

The "differend" of historical horror thus involves an ironic linkage of two sentences, one of which repudiates the possibility of faith and the other of which mitigates against the repudiation. The "idiom" or expression of historical horror consists of this setting up of oppositions that appears precisely at moments that call for resolution, replacing the satisfaction of resolution with the dissatisfaction of the refusal of such comfort. One could trace the same linkages as they appear in the poetry of Paul Celan, of Jacob Glatstein, of Abraham Sutzkever, of Dan Pagis, of Nelly Sachs.

The point I find significant here is the relationship between such a verbal juxtaposition and the experience to which it refers. The ironic "linkages" and other strategies that structure Wiesel's narrative are produced by, and therefore are linguistic evidence of, a vacuum in words created by events of historical horror. Words cannot encompass lived horror. It is precisely in its agonized technical and rhetorical play with their own muteness that words are witness to history. The philosopher Susan Shapiro, writes: "We must listen, therefore, not only to the "what" of their testimony, but to the witness of their language."[13] Lawrence Langer, James Young, and a host of other writers—the list is long—have analyzed in some depth the ways in which accounts of historical horror betray their very intention.[14] But these writers at times fail to note that the witnessing to historical horror does not occur in the telling, but in the inflection of the telling, in the formal consequences—the lapses, silences, omissions—that voice the horror that exceeds such telling. The professional readers and explicators seem often to adopt a position that strangely parallels the ultimately much more complicated rhetorical positions that lie at the heart of all testimony, poetry, and fiction of historical horror. The critical project of reading such a literature is not to add to a rhetoric of impossibility but to describe "the rules of formation and linkage" that are the conditions of testimony, that make testimony possible. It is to assist in the effort to make that testimony heard.

Chapter 5

The Literary Act of Witness:
Narrative, Voice, and the Problematic of the Real

> . . . the representational seeks continually to reshape and revi-
> talize ways of apprehending the actual, subjecting convention
> to an empirical review of its validity as a means of reproduc-
> ing reality. . . . But the representational is tied to the means of
> reproduction and varies as new ways of seeing or new artistic
> techniques of reproducing are discovered.
> —*Scholes and Kellogg*

Historical Horror and the Suspension of Disbelief

Wiesel and Conrad both call attention to the chasm that the
traumatic historical experience opens up between words and
fact, symbol and history, language and experience. Marlow
describes his feeling "bewitched and cut off forever from everything . . . amongst the overwhelming realities of this strange
world of plants, water and silence."[1] Similarly, Wiesel, describing deportation from the town of Sighet, describe his numbness
and sense of the unreal: "And there was I, on the pavement,
unable to make a move. . . . It was like a page torn from some

story book, from some historical novel about the captivity of Babylon or the Spanish Inquisition."[2]

The difficulty is clear: how to render an experience in all of its sensations and implications from which the mind must recoil, harden, deaden itself? In his pioneering study of trauma and mass death, Robert Lifton observes that:

> In order to dissociate itself from grotesque death the mind must itself cease to live, become itself deadened. The disassociation becomes intrapsychic in the sense that feeling is severed from knowledge or awareness of what is happening. . . .[3]

What is not really real can be safely confronted. The premise of disbelief upon which our relationship to the fictional world of narrative depends, breaks down where disbelief is already present. The pressure with which such a work must deal is precisely the pressure to counter the dissociation process, its threat to the self and to one's grasp of the world. "What is more basic," Lifton continues in the passage cited above, "is the self's being severed from its own history, from its grounding. . . ."

To explore such experience within fictional form threatens to perpetuate the dissociation process. To engage in a fictional procedure in coming to grips with historical catastrophe is to treat the actuality of traumatic historical experience as fiction and thereby to interfere with the goal of that telling. The writer who would write of such experiences writes out of a profound consciousness of this dissociation process, a process that undermines for the reader and for the writer alike the convention of "suspended disbelief" that is the shared, and also unwritten, understanding between the reader and writer.

The work of art that would represent historical horror is in a peculiarly complicated and vulnerable position. In Primo Levi's words: "To bear witness was an end for which to save oneself. Not to live and to tell but to live in order to tell."[4] Such a telling is no ordinary "telling." We ask that it tell us what cannot be told. We ask it to perform special communal and cultural tasks in society at large. We ask that it "bear witness" when art is founded on the very opposite notion of a "suspended disbelief" or separation between art and life. In the pages that follow, I will concern myself with two autobiographical novels, *Blood From the Sky* by Piotr Rawicz and *None of Us Shall Return* by Charlotte Delbo.[5] Rawicz's novel is the story of the decimation of his native town in the Ukraine. Delbo's novel, the first of a trilogy entitled *Auschwitz et Après*, is a rendering of the year Delbo spent as a political prisoner in Auschwitz.[6] The different technical procedures Rawicz and Delbo deploy in representing extreme experience will, I think, clarify the formal difficulties that face the writer who would represent historical horror. I hope such an examination will further demonstrate the formal connections that exist between an experience and the work of art, connections that, in Lyotard's words, "bear witness to differends by finding idioms for them."[7]

Piotr Rawicz: *Blood from the Sky*

"The purpose of eloquence," writes Frederick Hoffmann in *The Mortal No*, "is to direct the reader's attention away from fact," and he continues:

> or to link fact with one or several of the systems of larger meaning which in any period circumscribe fact. Eloquence also acts to slow the rhythm of factual succession. In key passages of classical drama, sequences of minor facts lead to a major fact: this latter requires a pause. . . . The more intensely violent fact becomes, the more solicitous is eloquence to mitigate its intensity.[8]

These observations bear upon Rawicz's novel up to a point. That point is the violent heart of the novel, a key scene upon which the first section of the novel, dealing with the liquidation of Rawicz's hometown in the Ukraine, closes. The rendering of the massacre involves the breaking down of the conventional character of narrated experience into separate, sequential passages of fact and eloquence, external event and subjective response, literal description and metaphor.

The breakdown of language proceeds out of a breakdown within the experiencing subject. "One comes to feel the self disintegrating at moments when one's inner forms and images become inadequate representations of the self-world relationship," Robert Lifton writes.[9] Words in this section, do not skirt so much as they stop short before horrific fact. Three off-duty soldiers hold Yaakov, one of a group of children accidentally discovered in hiding, while the Corporal cuts out his tongue with a bayonet that is too large for the purpose. "Not a word was uttered by the group of children, who froze into complete immobility. . . ." Violent detail unfolds in silence and in a factual, neutral, if ironic, tone that gives equal attention to the gouging of the eyes of another child and to the instrument used for the purpose, the "hornbacked penknife, the very one he used for opening tins of corned beef" (155).

The paragraph that follows this factual account of the action breaks the silence amid "indefinable noises, monstrous crossbred sounds," recording the sensations, skewed perceptions, and shattered meanings of these grotesque events in a language that is metaphorical, grammatically irregular, and outright metaphysical:

> They were slippery. They were trickly. Piercing screams filled the cellar. . . . Yawnings, indefinable noises, monstrous crossbred sound. Rendings of senses and skins. Geometric figures, geometry subsiding into madness. . . . The belly of the Universe, the belly of Existence was gaping open, and its filthy intestines were invading the room . . . and all astronomies were indulging in a masquerade or tussle, in a wedding or ride, and the stuff of dreams was sprawled on the Throne of God, who lay in a swoon on the concrete, surrounded by His own vomit. . . .   (155, 56)

The scene closes in a coda in which fact and eloquence come together to fight, in Hoffmann's words, "against the isolated factuality of fact." The protagonist, Boris, has returned to the scene of the massacred children with a nurse. She provides the dying children with injections to speed death. Images of gingerbread, cake, flowers, and sunshine associate the relief of death with a rhetoric of childhood and of idyll. Rawicz compares the nurse distributing death to the children to a gardener "who fulfills the destiny of the flowers and the sunshine by picking them":

> Several mutilated children were still suffering. The nurse went around distributing death, like portions of ginger-bread stuffed with darkness. For they do exist, Boris assures us, cakes stuffed with darkness. He also compares the nurse to the gardener who fulfills the destiny of the flowers and the sunshine by picking them.

The final passage is musical in the sense that it plays with experienced dissonance and employs diction, imagery, and metaphor to resolve the dissonance into a very different tonality: "For they do exist, cakes stuffed with darkness" (156).

The language of childhood belief into which the scene resolves mutes the violence of the earlier scene. The reader may, as it were, recover her breath, look past the disturbing implications of violent fact—escape. In Hoffmann's words, the purpose of eloquence is:

> to enable cultural implications to establish themselves, to distract the mind from the factual center, in short to allow the mind the chance to move away from the fact into the area of associative rhetoric.[10]

The sequence of passages discussed, then, captures the conflicting pressures to which language and narration are subject in the rendering of extreme violent fact. These pressures govern that rendering, its sequence and structure, no less than its texture, imagery, tonality.

But the issues are more complicated still. The account of the children's massacre is presented, not as part of a larger story, but apart from that story. It is an eyewitness account taken from a diary sent to the author. The interpolated diary account thus implicates a breakdown, not only at the level of language, but also of narration. To lay aside story is to lay aside the attempt to tell, at least in a novelistic sense.

Clearly, what is at stake is the issue of belief. As the narrative moves closer to the massacre scene, the contract undertaken by the reader to suspend disbelief in the fiction at hand cannot be sustained. The massacre as subject matter requires the belief of the reader, not in its fiction, but in its very facticity. What is required is a different contract altogether. Rawicz, understanding this need, lays aside the pretense and conventions of storytelling for a very different narrative posture: a posture of witnessing. The issue only grows more complicated, however, since the journal itself is described as "gibberish," highly edited, and, finally, unreliable. The account is a bracketed account. The point is the bracketing: the failure of a witnessed mode as well as of a narrative mode of telling.

The narration of traumatic historical events is thus caught on the warp of pressures both to tell and to disavow that telling, to integrate and to disintegrate, to establish factuality and, at the same time, to expose the fiction of that project, and in so doing, to recover the experience in its fragmentary nature.

Part one of Rawicz's novel is about the liquidation of a Ukrainian town. It ends with the massacre described above. Part two is about the escape and survival of the protagonist, Boris. The story of the liquidation is not rendered in a straightforward narration for all of its eighteen chapters. It begins as a story told from the point of view of Boris, who, in chapters 15, 16, and 17, leaves off his narrative of the last days of the ghetto and digresses in poetic, dramatic, and discursive modes on a variety of topics. The story resumes in chapter 18 by means of a newly introduced voice, that of the writer directly addressing the reader and speaking through the interpolated text of a diary—Boris's diary—mailed sometime after the war to the writer.

Narrative sequence, thus, seems to be a function of strategies designed to accommodate the factuality of violent fact in all of the ways that Hoffman suggests. The three chapters that separate the deportation of patients and staff of the ghetto hospital from the final brutal massacre of a hidden group of children do not recount the life of Boris or even provide us with information as to what is happening in the ghetto. Instead, they form a kind of pause in the narration, an empty space during which the last of the Jewish population is rounded up to be sent on to their deaths, a prose surface impervious to the violent facts that are recounted in partial and incomplete ways.

Chapter 15 begins on a note of anticipation. "Your narrator gets up, impelled by an indefinable feeling: a change of scene is about to happen." The writer describes Boris's voice, which has acquired a new roughness, and notes that dawn hangs back "in the grip of a stage fright so human. . . ." The reference to a fear associated with theater and performance is the mark of an unreality that invades and distorts the prosaic and familiar world: "A uniformed cop and your plain-clothes men keep lookout for the hesitant dawn. It fails to appear. It hangs back. . . ." Four pages later, the chapter closes and dawn appears:

> Whereupon, with his long, bony finger, Boris touches the paling sky. In one swift movement, he seemed to give a fleeting caress to the rising sun, petting it as though it were the lightest of balloons. . . .   (129)

The extended poetic lingering over the transition between day and night slows the temporal flow of the narrative both literally and musically. The hanging back of the sun refers first of all to the "hanging back" or pause which the reader experiences in the narrative, a lingering that inscribes the dread of the new day and of its violences into the slowed rhythms of the narrative.

> Oh, to drown, to annihilate this moment with the aid of words teeming like black insects. I dread Boris's fluency—certainly I do—but I dread even more what would happen if one now gave the sun free rein. (128)

Rawicz tells us that fluency (or "eloquence" in Hoffmann's terminology) is a means of staying time, of avoiding, if only briefly (and then only within the experienced temporal progression of the narrative), the horrors to come with dawn. The effect of a chapter about hanging back is to generate tension in the opposite direction: to build anticipation, to point to the violence from which words provide refuge and respite.

The next two chapters extend the pause of "Boris's fluency," or avoidance, at the same time that they address the anticipated moment of violence, its meanings, and its experience. Chapter 16 takes up the theme of language:

> One by one, words—all the words of the human language—wilt and grow too weak to bear a meaning. And then they fall away, like dead scales. All meanings evaporate. But that is their normal condition. Man grows dumb. . . .   (132)

Boris begins to speak (in his journal) about writing as though to disavow in advance his description of the violences that are already anticipated. "Yet more comparisons, yet more metaphors. It's enough to make one throw up" (132). And he laments:

> Between the terror inspired in me by a blank sheet of paper and the sense of shame that the aforesaid sheet gives off as soon as there are a few hasty marks on it, will there never be a "neutral zone". . . ?   (133)

The meditation on writing continues. Rawicz describes literature as "anti-dignity exalted to a system" (134). He attacks "literary manner," which "is an obscenity by definition," and compares the writer to an insect:

> . . . haven't you noticed that man never so much resembles an insect as when he engages in the activity of writing . . . ? Dissecting the world into tiny bits, covering paper with tiny scribbles that aspire to be unique. . . . And man's posture, and the movements of his brain at the time of writing—are they not those of an insect to end all insects, fleshy and pudgy. . . .   (134, 35)

Rawicz's references to selfhood and to a sense of the real suggest what Lifton calls a "coming apart of crucial components of the self."[9] In the same chapter, Rawicz writes that "Those actions in life which are reputedly . . . the most insignificant . . . strike me as being so much more . . . 'existent' than I, the supposed author of these notes" (132). A couple of pages later he comments that "The 'I' who had lived through the walled-up town and all the rest, is flowing away, draining away" (134). He describes a sense of non-being that fills him even as he writes:

> It is an especially revered deity, the deity of Nonentity, that jealously stays my hand. More and more seldom do I try to escape from it. For nonfulfillment is like soft fur. So, my brothers in Nothingness, fight Reality, crush it! There is no more degrading form of mass hypnosis. (133)

The disavowal of the writing activity, of self, and of reality in chapter 16 is followed, in chapter 17, by a description of Boris's journal, the journal from which author-cum-editor will fish out the account of the massacre in chapter 18. Rawicz ruminates on Boris's "mass of gibberish," on Boris's handwriting, on the linguistic hodgepodge of French, Slavonic, and other languages in which the journal is written. The voice that speaks at this point is that of the editor/author who complains about "a narrative in which I would have preferred . . . to see greater unity," and at another point that "the notes—even those I had been able to isolate after removing the pseudo-lyrical bits—were extremely muddled." The author, despite the condition of the manuscript, is tempted into salvaging a story that he describes as "the remains of a story which wasn't one, or wasn't quite. . . ." Thus, the narrative of the final death throes of the ghetto in chapter 18 is resumed, not as a story taken up once again, but on a new basis, as testimony.

But this "testimony" is itself tampered with, in drastic ways, by the author-cum-editor and hence, itself profoundly flawed:

> I have quoted from the manuscript wherever I was unable to do otherwise. I have summarized as often as seemed

possible, but first and foremost: I have CUT. And if I fancy
I have earned the right to any gratitude whatsoever from
any reader whatsoever—and I am in doubt as to that—it
will all be due to this wholesale amputating.

(140)

The documentary status of the account only complicates and
deepens our awareness of the gap between fact and account.
Even before reading it, we are informed that the account is
untruthful. Both chapters prepare the reader for the resumption
of the story of the ghetto's demise by disavowing that account
in advance. The disavowal occurs on the level of its explicit
thematization in chapter 16, and more playfully and formally in
chapter 17 with the device of the edited journal.

The two chapters are thus a formal consequence of the way
that violent fact destabilizes narrative. The pause, extending
over the three chapters that precede the massacre, consists of a
recognition of the subversive implications that are intrinsic to
the expression of violent fact. Not only does this pause of "eloquence" slow the pace of violent fact, the content of that "eloquence" is equally a function of the violent facts anticipated.

The novel thus calls attention to the issues raised by traumatic fact as a means of gaining access to those very facts. It calls
attention to violences done to our sense of the real, in order to
access the felt "realness," or facticity, of this violence. And it
calls attention to the fictionality of the fiction and of the eyewitness account as well, in order to recoup the experienced credibility of words in the same way that Pirandello's exposure of the
fictionality of the actors who play their roles in *Six Characters in
Search of an Author* affects the way we then experience his "characters." Pirandello plays with our belief in illusion in order to
generate, within the illusion and through its manipulation, a
very different kind of belief that stands on life, on experience, on
history. Through this formal manipulation, he plays with our
sense of the actual. For the space of the play we watch on stage,
he is able to reproduce a sensation of actuality different from
that of the illusions we have conventionally agreed to believe in.
Pirandello creates the illusion of something outside the illusion

of art. He helps us touch, as it were, the sense of a real outside artistic convention, outside a formal or "symbolic" reality.

Similarly, in the novel at hand, the dismantling of fictional convention and attack on storytelling in all of its fictional and nonfictional forms redraws the terms within which we then experience the horrific massacre. The appearance of utter confrontation with the lie of the fiction (a technique powerfully used in Lanzmann's *Shoah*) lends the horrific account the authority of that very truthfulness. If traumatic experience severs the self from its groundedness in experience, then reconstitution of a sense of the real must, paradoxically, be built upon an articulation of the very disjunctions that the traumatic experience produced.

The forms of language and of discourse called upon to speak about historical catastrophe are profoundly connected to the negating character of the experiences they would describe. Thus, it would seem that it is impossible to speak about violent fact without acknowledging the violence done to that very articulation. To write about such violence is to explore, in minute and intimate detail, the effect of that violence on the words that would describe it. The act of grasping violent fact in words must include, then, by formal definition, the action of grasping, in the most precise way possible, the exact boundaries of that description.

Expression and Voice: Charlotte Delbo's *None of Us Shall Return*

Charlotte Delbo is most fascinating for the technical virtuosity with which she approaches her subject.[11] *None of Us Shall Return* is written primarily as a stream-of-consciousness novel in the first-person plural. The "we" is the experiencing subject multiplied fifteen thousand times to include Delbo's historical comrades in suffering and in witnessing. Unlike Rawicz's novel, in which violent events determine the pace of the action, narrative sequence, rhythms, and content, Delbo's novel focuses on experiences rather than events. She writes chapters about thirst, about roll call, about nightmares, about a peasant cottage that offers shelter during a rain, about evening, about spring. Her chapters focus less on the extraordinary character of extremity than on the everyday aspect of extremity.

Delbo does not take her reader back to a historical account of an event, but rather to the experiencing communal consciousness in all of the fragmentation and instability of that experience, in its most intimate connection to the body, to the outer world, and to others. In this way, Delbo depicts that dissolution in all of its lived and witnessed precision. If the unreal lies at the heart of the experience of extremity, it is that unreal that achieves objective status in her account. What is formidable in her writing is the precision and detail of that portrait.

Whereas Rawicz, in order to write a narrative, shows us all the ways violent fact destabilizes narrative, Delbo constructs a voice that speaks and organizes a narrative from within that fragmented experience. Her concern is not a particular subject, but subjectivity under special conditions. She creates a form whose principle is phenomenological and descriptive. She records the dissonance of extreme experience and the violence it performs on notions of time, continuity, coherence, speaking, writing, signifying, and meaning. She uses a stream-of-consciousness technique in order to speak from within that dissonance as it affects the proper names of dead friends and the human response to the cries of a dying woman.

Delbo's account takes shape, not in the form of analogy, of telling, of narrative, but in a poetic unfolding of consciousnesss in particular situations, in physical sensation, and in the effects of these on human interactions. She is interested in providing us with the most minute data of such experiences: of thirst, of cold, of witnessing a beating, of the sight of a tulip, of sustaining oneself through roll call, of wishing to die, of nighttime, of dreams. She positions the reader within that consciousness and the operations it must perform upon the extreme experience of the death camp.

To give up narration, to give up story, is itself an acknowledgment of the limits of language and expression. Delbo thinks about story: Can she render thirst, for example, in the form of a story?

Thirst is an explorer's tale, you know, in the books we read as children. It is in the desert.

And she goes on to tell us the story as convention might have her tell it:

People who see mirages and walk toward the unattainable oasis. They are without water for three days. The pathetic chapter in the book. At the end of the chapter, the supply caravan arrives, it had gone astray on the trail obliterated by the sandstorm. The explorers break open the water bags, they drink. It is thirst from the sun, from the warm wind. The desert. A palm tree in filigree against the red sands.   (79)

Such is the thirst of convention, of story. But the thirst experienced by Delbo and her fifteen thousand women comrades who labor in the marshes of the death camp is different from the thirst in the story. It has no beginning, no middle, no foreseeable end:

But the thirst of the marsh is more burning than that of the desert. The thirst of the marsh lasts for weeks. The water bags never come. Reason wavers. Reason is laid low by thirst. Reason holds out against everything, but it gives in to thirst. In the marsh, no mirage, no hope of an oasis. Mud, mud. Mud and no water.   (79)

Delbo's chapter on thirst eschews story. Instead, it describes the effect of a dry mouth on the lips, the difficulty of speaking, the arrival of the tea canteen in the women's bunk before roll call:

They are not the water bags of the caravan. Quarts and quarts of herb tea, but divided into tiny portions, one each, and everyone else is still drinking when I am finished. My mouth is not even moistened and still the words refuse to come. My cheeks stick to my teeth, my tongue is hard, stiff, my jaws are blocked and still this feeling of being dead, of being dead and knowing it. And terror grows in my eyes. I feel terror growing in my eyes to the point of madness. Everything is sinking, everything is slipping away. . . .   (80)

She describes the obsession with thirst that lasts through the day, her inability to eat without saliva in the mouth, a dangerous attempt to get a cupful of water from a stream, the thirst of morning, afternoon and night:

> I have the taste of orange in my mouth, the juice seeps under my tongue, touches my palate, my gums, trickles down my throat. It is a slightly sour orange and wonderfully cool. This taste of orange and the sensation of cold wake me up. The awakening is dreadful. But the second when the orange peel gives between my teeth is so delightful that I would like to summon up that dream. I chase after it. . . .   (85)

Delbo's technical and philosophical choice to scrap narrative or story in favor of a stream of plural consciousness in a narrative present allows her to sidestep disbelief as a formal issue. She can thus move, in formal terms, from the elaboration of a negative statement (the impossibility and unreliability of the story) to a "positive," or content statement.

Where Rawicz pauses before the narration of the horrific massacre for the extraordinary length of three chapters, Delbo hovers over the violent instant itself. Her hovering is not a device, not a clever form of "telling but not telling," but a lingering in narrative time upon the violent fact itself and the conjunction of real and unreal that occurs with it.

In one passage she describes the dreams of night and the effort of consciousness to deny reality by investing dream with reality. A brick has come loose from a wall and the sleeper struggles to metamorphose the sensation of that brick into the stone sink of the home to which she returns each night in her dreams:

> We must go back, go back home to feel the sink stone with our hands and we fight against the vertigo that lures us to the bottom of the pit of night or of death. . . .
>   (63)

The dream state is not a state of fantasy, but a deeper state of freed awareness, awareness that has been numbed during the day so that it is in dream, rather than in a waking state, that the mind experiences the actuality of its experiences.

Delbo's sentences run on continuously, separated only by commas to indicate this deeper level in the flow of mind and perception. She lingers on the physical perception of the cold of the brick around which she organizes a host of nightmarish aspects of daily existence in which the brick is concretely implicated:

> . . . we make one last, desperate effort and we cling to the brick, the cold brick that we hold close to our heart, the brick that we have snatched from a pile of bricks stuck together with ice, chipping the ice with our nails, quick, quick, the clubs and the straps are flying—quick, quicker, our nails are bleeding—and this cold brick against our heart we carry to another pile, in a gloomy cortege in which each woman has a brick against her heart, for this is the way we carry bricks here, one brick after another. . . .   (63, 64)

The nightmare indeed consists of the details of the construction work at which the prisoners toil each day. Delbo's description of the sensation of a cold brick is the means by which she describes both the external reality of the inhuman work to which the prisoners are consigned and the inner reality of its traumatic character. For all of its poetic organization, the passage is very literal, even commonsensical, in its observations of the ways the construction site invades the "rest" of night as well as in its evocation of yet more detail of that real concentration camp universe that is Auschwitz:

> . . . from morning till evening and it is not enough that we must carry bricks all day long at the construction site, we carry them again at night, for at night everything pursues us at once, the mud of the marsh in which we sink, the cold bricks that we must carry against our hearts, the kapos who shout and the dogs who can move

> in the mud as on solid ground and bite us at a signal
> from the flashing eyes in the darkness and we have the
> hot moist breath of the day on our faces and fear beads
> our temples.   (64)

What we are given is not a story about the terrors of working at the construction site but terror as it is freed by a brick that has come loose from the wall. The brick acts as a trigger to the consciousness of the sleeper, releasing suppressed and horrific detail of the real concentration camp world that stands outside that consciousness but that has also invaded it. The dreamer seeks in the brick, the materiality of the real that is radically undermined by historical extremity. The passage encapsulates the dilemma of a consciousness that must numb itself to the assault of daily existence but that in so doing, sustains profound wounds to its vital link to a real world that is the ground of speaking, writing, living.

The brick image is drawn out of the nightmare of the real. It is a physical sign of that concentrationary world, a sign, not analogous to, but physically drawn from the daily routine at the construction site:

> the brick that we have snatched from a pile of bricks
> stuck together with ice . . . quick, quick, the clubs and the
> straps are flying . . . this cold brick . . . we carry to another
> pile . . . for this is the way we carry bricks here, one brick
> after another, from morning till evening. . . .   (63, 64)

At the same time, the passage addresses another dimension of the brick: it is a brick "that we hold close to our heart . . .":

> and we cling to the brick, the cold brick that we hold
> close to our heart
>
> and this cold brick against our heart . . . in which each
> woman has a brick against her heart
>
> the cold bricks that we must carry against our hearts
>   (63, 64)

The brick that is carried "against our heart" is also a lifeline to a world outside the mind. Its coldness is all too real. Delbo's sentences zigzag from inner to outer bricks:

> the cold brick that we hold close to our heart, the brick
> that we have snatched from a pile of bricks   (63)

> in which each woman has a brick against her heart, for
> this is the way we carry bricks here   (64)

The brick is invoked again and again as though its repetition would aid us in grasping the very materiality of the brick; as though the materiality of the brick could unlock a thwarted consciousness, bring comfort to the numbed heart. The dreamer seeking to "go home, go back home, to feel the sink stone with our hand," makes "one last desperate effort," an effort that takes the form of clinging to the brick:

> We feel ourselves teetering over a pit of shadow, a bottomless pit—it is the pit of night or of another nightmare, or our real death, and we struggle furiously, endlessly. We must go back, go back home to feel the sink stone with our hands . . . we make one last, desperate effort and we cling to the brick. . . .   (63)

The linguistic form of the passage is a kind of clinging as well. The organization of the passage around the brick, the repetition of the brick, the zigzagging between inner and outer bricks are the means by which Delbo conveys the lived "sensation of things as they are perceived and not as they are known. . . ."[12] By means of a stream-of-consciousness rendering, she allows the traces of that experience to mark her narrative and reveal the altered ways that consciousness experiences itself under extreme conditions.

In *At the Mind's Limit*, Jean Améry writes of the difficulty of finding words for bodily extremity:

> It would be totally senseless to try and describe the pain that was inflicted on me. Was it "like a red-hot iron in my shoulders," and was another "like a dull wooden

stake that had been driven into the back of my head"? One comparison would only stand for the other, and in the end we would be hoaxed by turn on the hopeless merry-go-round of figurative speech. The pain was what it was. Beyond that there is nothing to say. Qualities of feeling are as incomparable as they are indescribable. They mark the limit of the capacity of language to communicate. If someone wanted to impart his physical pain, he would be forced to inflict it and thereby become a torturer himself.[13]

Améry insists that "Qualities of feeling are as incomparable as they are indescribable." There are no words that can substitute for the exact qualities of feeling. In chapter 16, Rawicz similarly suggests that violent fact involves a perceived breakdown of the ability of words to stand for things, dirty cotton for grey clouds, the mere telling or story of the destruction of a town in the Ukraine for the fact of its destruction:

> With rusty scissors, I used to cut up bits of the sky. I used to compare clouds to dirty cotton, easy as preparing boiled eggs. . . . Yet more comparisons, yet more metaphors. It's enough to make one throw up.   (132)

Both Rawicz and Delbo use a metaphor of organic death to describe the effect of extreme experience on words. "One by one, words—all the words of the human language—wilt and grow too weak to bear a meaning" Rawicz writes (132) and Delbo writes: "All words have wilted long ago" (126). And she describes the efforts of the women to carry the bodies of their dead friends back to the camp:

> At first it is Berthe and Ann-Marie that we are carrying. Soon they are nothing more than very heavy bundles that slip out of our grasps at every movement.   (90)

The story of the ways that proper names are transformed into "very heavy bundles that slip out of our grasps at every moment" is a literal description of a psycholinguistic process, a dissolving, under conditions of extremity, of the human beliefs and connections that make the connections between word and thing possible. As experience exceeds the possibility of integrating or containing it, naming becomes increasingly impossible. Delbo focuses, not on names, words and story, but on the connections that sustain them in the process of their dissolution.

At one point Delbo writes of watching trucks pass filled with other women who, in a short space of time, will be gassed and burned: "The living shrink with fear. With fear and revulsion. They shriek. We hear nothing." The experiencing self wards off the words of the doomed, cannot hear or respond to those words, and Delbo addresses herself to that deafness: "We hear nothing. The truck glides silently over the snow. . . ." Delbo places before us the fragmenting nature of the experience by juxtaposing the exactness and intensified seeing of the witness with the deafness to which it is deeply allied:

> We watch with eyes that cry out, that do not believe.
> Each face is inscribed with such precision in the icy light, on the blue of the sky, that is marked there for eternity.   (39)

What is privileged in this passage is the consciousness that is the consequence of, and response to, violent fact. The facts are minimal—women pass in trucks, cry out, the trucks disappear. But they are also disorienting:

> The women pass near us. They cry out. They cry out and we hear nothing. This cold and dry air would be conductive if we were in an ordinary earthly environment. They cry out to us but no sound reaches us. Their mouths cry out, their outstretched arms cry out, and every bit of them cries out. Each body is a cry. So many torches that flame in cries of terror, so many cries that have assumed the bodies of women. Each woman is a materialized cry, a scream that is not heard. The truck moves silently over the snow, passes under a portico, disappears. It carries off the cries.   (39)

This passage records the shared consciousness of the living who hear, and who are defended from hearing, the cries of the doomed. The pause of "eloquence" is poised specifically on the question of hearing, that is, on the question of the effect of extremity on perception. The "eloquence" or language that fills the written spaces between the arrival and departure of the women in the trucks does not focus away from violent fact. It suspends that violence over narrated time.

The crying out is repeated in slightly different form each time. The life energy soon to be extinguished seems to locate itself in those cries, cries that, in the course of the passage, acquire bodies. At first the cries are merely soundless: "They cry out to us but no sound reaches us." Then the passage records the cry visually: "Their mouths cry out, their outstretched arms cry out." Finally we are told that the bodies of the women have dematerialized into cries: "Each body is a cry." The next sentence involves a reversal in which the cry is transformed into a body: ". . . so many cries that have assumed the bodies of women." Finally, the cry that had become body dissolves back into unheard cry: "Each woman is a materialized cry, a scream that is not heard. The truck moves silently. . . . It carries off the cries."

It is the bounded physical presence of all of those bodies marked for immediate extermination that moves the reader as the cry, in its very insubstantiality, in its fragility, in the brief history of its presence, appears only to disappear. The cry that cries out ever more urgently only to fade away into silence, projects a materiality of the body that anticipates this very fate, this fading into nothing and silence.

The relation of cry and body forms the heart of the passage. The metaphor is unstable and that seems to be its point. The women and the cries are at first disconnected from one another in the consciousness of Delbo and the other witnesses. The women then become cries. The cries also become bodies. As the passage closes the cries and bodies once again detach in the consciousness of the witnesses. At no point are they in a conventional relationship in which one stands for the other or substitutes for the other. Their connection seems to have nothing whatever to do with analogy and everything to do with the ways that the human body experiences itself—its materiality and immateriality, its crushing presence and threatened absence—under conditions of extremity. There is an exchange, as it were, between body and voice that occurs at the heart of the passage and toward which the passage moves.

This exchange involves the identifications and hearing against which Delbo and her comrades are defended. The repetition of the unheard cry locates the unheard in the strange trajectory of that cry—in the tenuousness of body and voice, in the relation of real and unreal; in the organicity of the one and in the insubstantiality of the other.

Exactness and the Literal Surreal

In eschewing story, Delbo eschews the presumption of a correspondence between language and experience that is the ground of formal expression. Instead, she develops an extraordinary language of exactness in representing the human being in extremity.

Under conditions of extremity, incoming stimuli are dulled in some ways, distorted in other ways. Here is Delbo's description of marching in bitter cold to work:

> . . . but the cold is so intense that we no longer feel it. Before us sparkles the plain: the sea. We follow. The ranks cross the road, move straight toward the seas. In silence. Slowly. Where are we going? We move onward into the sparkling plain. We move onward into the light solidified by the cold. The S.S. shout. We do not understand what they shout. The columns strike out into the sea, farther and farther into the icy light. . . .   (36)

Delbo makes clear the way that traumatic experience, in this case the intense cold, interferes with the ways we see and understand, with the ways we experience space, cold, sound, and light. She records the ways that the body in extremity begins to experience itself in its parts, the way that the parts no longer seem to be part of a whole, the way that vitality gives way to numbness, and the mind itself seems to shut down:

So numb that we seem to be only a chunk of cold. . . .
Our legs move as if they were not part of us.   (36)

Not that we feel colder, we just become more and more
inert, more and more unfeeling.

We watch without comprehending.

. . . we have lost all the senses of life.   (38)

Delbo's extreme faithfulness, a clinical faithfulness, in
recording the effects of extremity on the perceptual process,
specifically here the effect of extreme cold on fifteen thousand
women, has the poetic effect of creating the sense of a reality
that is other, that is detached from the mundane, that is different, heightened. It creates the poetic effect of a literal surreal:

We are frozen fast in a hard block of ice as transparent as
a block of crystal. And this crystal is bathed in light, as
though light were frozen in ice, as though the ice were
light.   (37)

The experience of cold takes the form of key images, images of ice,
hardness, light, time, transparency, and embeddedness, which in
turn provide the organizing images of the larger chapter.

The passage describes the perceptual process under intense
assault, the ways that it detaches from experience and under-
goes a kind of reorganization on a perceptual level: cold is not
felt but seen (witnessed) and also associated with light. The
experience of cold involves an embeddedness. The women are
"frozen fast in a hard block of ice." The ice is hard but also "as
transparent as a block of crystal." Delbo remains with the image
of the crystal and plays with its quality of transparency that permits light to filter through: "And this crystal is bathed in
light. . . ." The features of the imagined block of ice in which the
women feel themselves to be embedded, its hardness and its
transparency, merge. The density of the encasing ice collapses
into the insubstantiality of the light: "as though light were
frozen in the ice, as though the ice were light."

The final lines of the paragraph capture the essential experience of coldness and, through it, of extremity. Delbo extends the contrast of ice and light, of density and immateriality that is part of the coldness to the women's experience of the self. To exist inside such coldness, inside the block of ice, is also to cease to exist in some perceptual and existential sense:

We do not know if we exist, only ice, light dazzling snow, and us, in this ice, in this light, in this silence. (37)

The experiencing self has undergone a dissolution under the onslaught of stimuli. What remains, and what Delbo is at great linguistic pains to describe, are the qualities of a cold so cold that nothing exists but that coldness. Surface or aesthetic play with the notion of coldness is play with a coldness whose severity implicates the dissolution of the experiencing subject.

I am suggesting that Delbo's technical procedures produce an aesthetic surface upon which a breakdown within the experiencing subject is inscribed. A precise, poetic language that describes concrete, overwhelming, and traumatic experiences builds its associational play around textures of an experience and a psychic economy that are radically other from what obtains in more usual circumstances. More specifically, where extreme experience renders an experience unavailable (numbing, coldness), poetic language marks the numbing, exploits the fragmenting of the perceptual process, and dwells on perceptual facts that mark the disintegration of the experiencing self within the experience. It is as though cold, where it cannot be experienced via its natural route, is then experienced via an alternative route, that is, visually. Metaphor, in this case the block of ice/crystal, is the record of such a process in perception, of the effort of the organism to reintegrate experience along alternative pathways. It is not analogous to experience in the sense of Améry's "hopeless merry-go-round of figurative speech" but extends and intensifies a clinical exactness. Poetic language in *None of Us Shall Return* is a means of describing consciousness. Delbo's poetic method is a tool of the analysis of experience. Poetic language, in other words, is a literal transcription and elaboration of perceptual processes and experience.

Language and Witnessing

As much as Rawicz and Delbo approach conventions of narration differently, they are each profoundly involved with the same questions. Leo L., head of the ghetto, says to Boris and Naomi before they leave the Jewish ghetto for a brief sojourn outside its walls:

> "Of you who are leaving, a few may survive, I am by no means certain. But should you happen to do so, remember everything, remember carefully. Your life will be no life. You are going to become strangers to yourselves and to everyone else. The only thing that matters, that WILL matter, is the integrity of the witnesses. Be witnesses, and God keep you. . . ."   (27)

The notion of "witness" emphasizes words, not in the adequacy of their representational function but as faithful indices of memory, inerrant markers of historical events. It bypasses the problem of word and thing by treating words not as names for things, flawed attempts to describe things and events that cannot be described, but as testimony or evidence on their behalf. The purpose of testimony is to authenticate fact: to locate fact in history and establish its facticity. The concern with witnessing in works about historical catastrophe involves the need for a mode of speaking capable of anchoring the "exploded bits of reality" that elude and break down before violent fact.[14] Conrad's *Heart of Darkness* skirts the devastations of the imperialist venture in Africa at the same time that it is structured around Marlow's journey to receive the testimony of Kurtz. The power of Kurtz's famous words, "'The horror! The horror!'" does not have to do with the word "horror" but with its witnessed, testimonial force. "Kurtz had judged. He had summed up."

Delbo employs notions of witnessing in her narrative in ways very different from Conrad and Rawicz. If in Rawicz the witnessed account finally breaks down before the facticity to which it cannot bring formal testimony, the connection between experience and language remains intact in Delbo. Delbo evolves a language of clinical precision in *None of Us Shall Return*, in which the flow of words, of rhythmic, and of associational play evolve out of—and are thereby witness to—events of historical horror and trauma.

Delbo's treatment of time is fundamental to the ways in which her writing is marked by extreme experience. Narrative time in *None of Us Shall Return* unfolds within the subjective logic and temporal rhythms of the wounded body. "The will to struggle and resist, life, had taken refuge in a reduced part of the body, just the immediate vicinity of the heart," she writes (29). At another point she writes:

> What is nearer to eternity than a day? What is longer than a day? How can one know that it is passing? Clod follows clod, the furrow moves back, the carriers continue their rounds.   (54)

Words like "eternity," "immobility," and "motionlessness" are repeated throughout Delbo's text to suggest the totalizing aspect of traumatic experience. Delbo writes of the terrifying screams of women being taken to the gas chambers, screams that do not disappear with the women but that are somehow caught and reverberate forever in time: "The screams remain inscribed on the blue of the sky" (39). She describes the faces of the women: "Each face is inscribed with such precision on the icy light, on the blue of the sky, that it is marked there for eternity." Describing the painful dying of a woman, Delbo notes the slowing of perceptual time as well as the stillness of the women who witness that dying:

> Suddenly a shiver runs through this heap that the yellow coat makes in the slush. The woman is trying to get to her feet. Her actions break down into unbearable slow motion. She kneels, looks at us. None of us move. . . . (32)

Physical immobility is perceptually linked to the experience of a collapsing temporality. "And we remain standing in the snow. Motionless in the plain" (34). The motionlessness of a "time outside of time" (37) that is explicitly referred to again and again is inscribed into the novel by a narrative present from which Delbo traces the flowing consciousness of a communal "we."

The narrative present of extreme experience is the present of an endlessly disintegrating instant. The disintegrating instant always evokes awareness of its disintegration:

> The light is still immobile, wounding, cold. It is the light of a dead star. And the vast frozen expanse, infinitely dazzling, is that of a dead planet.   (38)

Words like "star," and "infinitely dazzling," remind us of a light that is associated with insight, transparency, and radiance within a description of a very different sense of light. That light, experienced by fifteen thousand women prisoners while at work on a bitter cold morning, is "immobile," "wounding," and "cold." Immobility is thus a physical experience of these women's bodies even as it is connected to the structure of the traumatic experience.

Such a context severely undermines the conventions of "associated rhetoric" of which Hoffman writes in which light, for example, is associated with transcendence. "It is the light of a dead star," Delbo writes. Thus the immobility that is connected to the cold experienced by fifteen thousand women and perceptually linked to the experience of a collapsing temporality, takes the form in Delbo of an imagery of negated transcendence ("dead planet"), of obstructed movement, of vital energy unable to engage itself, unable to find words:

> Immobile in the ice in which we are caught fast, inert, unfeeling, we have lost all the senses of life. No one says: "I am hungry. I am thirsty. I am cold."   (38)

Extremity erases a tension between the life of the body and the life of the mind. Structures supplied by consciousness that mitigate against the mortality of the body disappear—or almost disappear. That disappearance is the mark of extreme experience. On the last pages of the novel, memories of spring interfere with the life of mind and body in extremity. "It is . . . harder to die when the sun is shining," Delbo writes:

Spring sang in my memory—in my memory.
This song surprised me so much that I was not sure
that I heard it. I thought I was hearing it in a dream. And
I tried to deny it, not to hear it and I cast a despairing
glance at my companions around me. . . .

Memory brings consciousness and language of another kind:

And in my memory spring was singing. . . .
Silvery pussywillows sparkled in the sun—a poplar
bends in the wind—the grass is so green that the spring
flowers shimmer with surprising colors. Spring bathes
everything in a light, light intoxicating air. Spring goes to
one's head. Spring is a symphony bursting forth on
every side, bursting, bursting.
Bursting. In my bursting head.   (124)

The bursting that is associated with spring and its physical
bounty involves an expanding motion of consciousness. The
final sentence reverses that consciousness in favor of another
one, a consciousness that is marked by an image of violent physical head pain.

The repetition of the word "bursting" modulates between
these two kinds of consciousness and between two directions in
language, from an imagery associated with burgeoning life
forces to a bodily image of puncture, pain, and contraction. The
collapse of an outward lyrical flow of awareness into an image
of body is similar to the unheard cries of the women that metamorphose into bodies and to the light that is frozen in the ice.
More globally, it is part of a movement toward density and facticity of body that negates impulses toward meaning and transcendence connected in memory and language to a different
form of consciousness.

"Transported to another world," Delbo writes, "we are at the
same time exposed to the breath of another life, to living death.
In ice, in light, in silence" (38). The poetic effect of the closing
words of this passage has to do with their links to a complex of
meanings that collapse under the weight of overwhelming and

traumatic experience. At a different point, the sight of stars and of a barbed-wire fence is experienced through the body rather than beheld by the eyes:

> I do not look at the stars. They stab with cold. I do not look at the barbed-wire fences lit up in the dark. They are claws of cold.   (72)

Delbo inscribes a language of the body within that other, more metaphysical, more familiar language. To turn away from stars that "stab with cold," that "are claws of cold," is to bring witness of this other, more familiar, language to the witness of body.

Rawicz and Delbo evolve two different modes within which to explore the historical catastrophe. Rawicz writes, finally, about the breakdown of formal truth. Delbo evolves a writing style that is able to maintain an authentic, experienced connection to the subject of which she writes. Her decision to scrap narrative in favor of a stream of plural consciousness in a narrative present allows Delbo to evolve structures of meaning, imagery, and surface texture which flow out of the traumatic experience. Delbo's prose poetry is a poetry of witnessing in the strict sense that the connection between the experience and its rendering is never broken.

In writing about "the witness of poetry," in his collection of essays under that title, Czeslaw Milosz defines poetry as a "passionate pursuit of the Real":

> I have defined poetry as a "passionate pursuit of the Real." . . . That elementary contact, verifiable by the five senses, is more important than any mental construction. The never-fulfilled desire to achieve a mimesis, to be faithful to a detail, makes for the health of poetry. . . . The very act of naming things presupposes a faith in their existence and thus in a true world, whatever Nietzsche might say.[15]

Delbo's technical inventiveness and exquisite writing style make possible the very exchanges between language and experience of which other narratives of "historical horror" uniformly despair.

Chapter 6

Concluding Thoughts and Promptings

Extremity is not new and neither is our response to it. In a lecture on the history of the concept of trauma, Bessel van der Kolk traced the way that the concept of trauma surfaces and then repeatedly disappears throughout the twentieth century.[1] He noted that the first medical studies of trauma begin at Salpetrier with the lecture demonstrations on hysteria by the French neurologist Jean-Martin Charcot, a line of investigation that continues with Breuer, Freud, and Janet.[2] Concepts of dissociation and distinctions between ordinary and traumatic memory made by Janet and others, reappear during the First World War only to be laid aside, and resurface when work with survivors of the Holocaust, of extreme domestic and sexual abuse, and of Vietnam brings renewed attention to the study of trauma. "Repression, dissociation, and denial are phenomena of social as well as individual consciousness," Judith Herman explains in *Trauma and Recovery*.[3] Indeed, the more radical insights of Robert Lifton, who, in *The Broken Connection* rethinks psychoanalytic theory of human development and personality based on extensive on-site studies of trauma and exposure to mass death in Hiroshima, are never picked up and fully explored although some of the more recent work in literary and trauma studies acknowledges its debt to Lifton.[4]

The history of the concept of trauma, in other words, bears within it the partial recognitions and suppressions that are typical of traumatic symptomatology itself. *Heart of Darkness* incorporates this ambivalence and doubleness around radical traumatic knowledge in Marlow's splitting of his testimony: he bears witness to Kurtz's testmony and brings that testimony to his companions on board the *Nellie* but he bears false witness to Kurtz's Intended and suppresses knowledge of Kurtz's nature and behavior in the Congo. In bringing us this act of suppression, Conrad predicts our own rather remarkable suppression of Congolese history—the full extent of which has recently come to public attention with the publication of Adam Hochschild's *King Leopold's Ghost*.[5] In effect, Conrad foresaw the wayward critical and interpretive history of his own text. Hochschild calls the suppression of Congolese history "the great forgetting," and, in an article that appeared in the *The New Yorker*, he chides criticism for overlooking the historical occasion and preoccupation of *Heart of Darkness*:

> Writers and academics have looked at the novel in terms of Freud and Jung and Nietzsche, of Victorian innocence and original sin, of patriarchy and Gnosticism, of postmodernism and post-colonialism and post-structuralism. But as hundreds of monographs and Ph.D. theses pour out, with titles like "The Eye and the Gaze in 'Heart of Darkness': a Symptomological Reading," it is easy to forget that the novel was closely based on a real place and time. . . .[6]

If the history of *Heart of Darkness* and its interpretation reflects this suppression, does a similar blind spot enter the critical vocabularies we have developed to describe and write about literature and language? In his book, *The Survivor: An Anatomy of Life in the Death Camps*, Terrence Des Pres muses on the familiar figure of the tragic hero and its role in the pervasive and well-nigh invisible cultural suppression of radical traumatic knowledge:

We may . . . find that one of the functions of culture is to provide symbolic systems which displace awareness of what is terrible, and that through death the hero takes upon himself the condition of victimhood and thereby grants the rest of us an illusion of grace. . . . The problem now is that symbolic manipulations of consciousness no longer work. Death and terror are too much with us.[7]

We need to look more carefully at the critical and analytic vocabulary with which we describe and digest our own narratives of extreme experience. As I mull the pages of this book, I see a large, virtually virgin terrain of narrative—the narrative of unrepresentability—which needs to be examined, a terrain for which, like Africa at the time of Conrad's voyage, there is no map drawn as yet. My own reading of *Heart of Darkness* views Conrad as taking up this very question of two utterly different orders or fields of narrative: the narrative of familiar experience or what I call the representable, and the narrative of extreme experience or what I have called, the unrepresentable.

In chapter 1, I draw the obvious distinction between literary horror associated with the gothic and macabre, and literary horror that attempts to bring us the extreme experiences of history. The lack of such a distinction speaks to kinds of imprecision and blurring that occur in literary discussions of these works which casually lump silences of historical trauma, catastrophe, and extreme experience with the philosophical silences of a post-philosophical and theorizing age. We are left with a critical vocabulary that replicates the dissociation and memory lapses which Janet, then Freud, Lifton, van der Kolk, Judith Herman, and so many others have described with frightening clinical precision. Conrad hammers home the thesis in *Heart of Darkness* that language is complicit with evil. Symbolic and critical evasion of the nature of traumatic experience and of its expression facilitates the slippages of knowing that make repetition of horror easier.

Words, Frederick Hoffmann tells us, are often used to mitigate and help us escape the experience that threatens.[8] To name is, to some extent, like taking a snapshot of a ship that has finally come into view. The ship is captured in the snapshot, its outlines preserved and frozen, even though it has sailed on to other ports, lies anchored, perhaps, or already has been retired from service and no longer exists as it did once. And thus, with the snapshot, the view of the ship is preserved but also removed from the life-world, altered, destroyed, and something else substituted. The word, like the snapshot, is but a substitute for things in experience that continually move in and out of our line of vision. Like the snapshot, words provide us with powerful illusions of our experiences.

Like a series of snapshots (e.g., a snapshot of the ship first appearing on the horizon, a full-view snapshot, a snapshot of the ship disappearing on the horizon), a story or narrative provides a powerful illusion of the trajectory of an experience. The illusion is different from the experience, is informed by the experience, and, indeed, is in dialogue with the experience. But, it is not the experience. It is separate from the experience.

Let us imagine a very different kind of experience. This experience has fuzzy outlines. It seems to lose the temporal structure—beginning, middle, and end—that allows us to make sense of the experience, to put it into words, to communicate it to others. It is an experience that has, as it were, fallen out of time, spills over and across time, and no longer exists within time or, even, one might say, within the experiencing subject. Having fallen out of time, it also has fallen out of language. The experience is neither tragic, comic, nor epic. It is not narrative, dramatic, poetic, discursive, allegorical, symbolic, or ironic. It is none of these because it has no words and cannot be framed into words. There is no snapshot to be taken because this ship never emerges into view. What shapes do words take in the absence of words?

This is the question that criticism has yet to look at steadily and with care. For there are shapes. There is a snapshot—a snapshot which foregrounds the empty space in which the ship was to appear, should have appeared and does not appear. The snapshot may even have accompanying text that will explain how this picture of an absent ship came to be taken. The picture, in other words, will bring us two stories, one told and one untold, a story of omission and a story of substitution. What we need to analyze as carefully as we might analyze the way a particular metaphor operates in a complicated poem, is exactly how this absence operates (since it involves no pictures or words, it stands for nothing, and yet it does open up something, does it not?). Aharon Appelfeld's *Badenheim 1939* omits the genocide that will swallow the lives of the Jews of Badenheim and tells the story of a music festival that cannot take place, of people who know but also do not know the fate that awaits them. The historical horror of anticipated genocide is left wordless. Yet, a whole secondary, surrealistic, and charged narrative is woven around questions that have to do with an epistemology of historical horror: the musical theme and narrative of Badenheim's music festival is an oblique way of asking questions about speaking, expressing, knowing, and not knowing. An identical double structure obtains in *Heart of Darkness* in which the story told is the story of Marlow's journey to receive Kurtz's testimony to "the horror," and the story of the horror, a story that is never fully told. Similarly, the film *Shoah* foregrounds an absence of words: spaces created where the stories of survivors break down. The stories recorded on film are the personal journeys of each survivor to retrieve memories, the most awful of which cannot be transformed into words.

It is as though these works involve themselves in the most fascinating paradox of all. They use a verbal structure in such ways as to make formally available an erasure of speech: to bring me, the reader or the viewer, the possibility of (or, at the very least, the assertion of) experiences that cannot be mediated by words. Or, better, they enact a dying or erasure of words so that in the blank of the space created, the real horror—that which always remains outside words—can begin to be heard.

Unlike the experience of historical horror, unrepresentability in narrative and in art is neither mysterious nor incapable of analysis. It is complex and involuted, since it involves the creation of textual and imaginative space in which the key event is a failure of symbolic systems and manipulation, a failure of the simplest narrative act, metaphor, mere word itself, to address and represent its subject. The impossibility at issue is not rhetorical but substantive. It is the key formal and structural problem that confronts the writer with every choice he or she faces in the wording and shape of a text: how to use form in such a way as to enact a breakdown of form.

What exactly occurs within such a breakdown; what does it consist of formally and aesthetically? To erase words, to bring the silence of that erasure to a reader or viewer, is to remove mediating symbols and create a space, but also a vulnerability to trauma. If the ship—or, more accurately, the image of the ship in the snapshot and therefore its illusion—does not, in this scenario, come into view, the absence is not a symbol; it is not another illusion. It is other and it is outside the play of symbolic form; it is outside the interchange of experience and language, of language and silence. In its aesthetic character, it partakes of and participates in, the failure of symbolic forms that is created by extreme experience. To be touched by such an absence or silence is to experience a hole in the fabric of language, a hole and not a symbol of a hole, a hole that is the effect of extreme traumatic experience, even if not the experience itself.

I have referred to a "hole in the fabric of language" having in mind Robert Brinkley and Steven Joura's acute analysis of Claude Lanzmann's *Shoah*. In "Tracing *Shoah*," Brinkley and Joura use the Peircian notion of indexicality to understand the Lanzmann film.[9] They cite the philosopher, Charles Sanders Peirce: "(Something) with a shot in it is a sign of a shot . . . whether or not anybody has the sense to attribute it to a shot or not," and explain that:

> . . . a bullet hole is a sign that a gun was fired. As an index, the sign is not determined by the interpretation; it is determined historically, by the event that produced it.

> . . . an index is constituted "in some existential relation to the object." . . .   (143)

The "hole in the fabric of language" or—in *Shoah*, the repeated breakdown of the stories of survivors—is a sign of historical trauma in a manner that is different from the way that an image or word is a sign or substitution for its referent. Traumatic narratives are structurally dissimilar from narrative as we conventionally understand it because such narratives have an existential and indexical, instead of merely a "representational," relationship to their subject. The hole to which I refer, the breakdown of the very possibility of symbol-making, is the consequence of the experience of historical trauma and horror irrespective of, and prior to any and all interpretation. Thus the black hole or horror at the center of Conrad's *Heart of Darkness* is indexically and existentially linked to the catastrophic events of Leopold in the Congo, regardless of a long and extraordinary history of critics who overlook the connection of Conrad's catastrophic subject matter to the peculiar narrative structure and design of that work.

Brinkley and Joura write of "the referential force that Peirce calls the 'indexical,'" a force that they show informs *Shoah* and its detail. They show the ways the film documents a persistence of the traces of genocide precisely where erasures were attempted: the ways that trees that were intended to conceal a death camp become evidence in *Shoah* of the killings they had been planted to hide; the ways that the memory lapses of the deputy commissioner of Warsaw, when confronted with the diary of Adam Czerniakow, turn into evidence (110). My point is related but not identical: I am suggesting that "the referential force that Peirce calls the 'indexical'" informs not only the details of *Shoah*, but also its shape and the shape of all attempts to put events into words that are themselves like the gunshot that makes a "hole in the fabric of language." For the purposes of criticism, we might indeed say that a work of historical horror—a film like *Apocalypse Now*, *Saving Private Ryan*, *Life Is Beautiful*, or *Europa Europa*—is aesthetically successful to the extent that it is able to give visibility and "referential force" to the "hole" of unrepresentability.

Shoah does not merely bring us witness after witness to the events of the Holocaust, but is crafted from within what Brinkley and Joura call "a discourse of witness," a system of relations that is existential and indexical and that involves the viewer "in the work of bearing witness":

The witness also interprets, necessarily—but with the understanding that interpretation can never grasp what it can only barely sustain, the irrevocable connection between sign and referent, the indexical imperative of the sign.   (125)

The notion of witness, in this view, includes a very different relationship of the viewer to a film, of the reader to a literary work; it includes the creation of an existential, and not merely vicarious, relationship to the work of art.[10] And it includes the recognition that the very form taken by such a work of art is an effect of the nature of the traumatic.

If storytelling claims to tell a story that bears resemblance to a reality, witnessing makes no such claim on behalf of language. It does not claim a representational truth. It claims a truth of having seen or been present in an historical and existential, rather than in a simulated, linguistic reality. Witnessing becomes important where events have outstripped imagination and the laws of credibility so that representation itself becomes impossible. As a literary device, witnessing is a means of implicating "the hole in the fabric of language." Marlow's journey to hear Kurtz's testimony, the construction of *Shoah* around witnessing that exposes the "hole in the fabric of language," the continual falling apart of storytelling and of documentary witnessing in Rawicz's *Blood from the Sky*, Wiesel's famous oath of witnessing in *Night*, Delbo's evolution of a language of clinical exactitude for her Auschwitz experiences that ironically and poignantly relinquishes the symbol-making dimensions of language—all of these narrative and aesthetic strategies extend out of a principle or mode of witnessing that assumes importance precisely where representation is no longer possible.

In chapter 3, I write of the coming apart or disruption of the "exchange between language and experience" that occurs with the experience of historical horror or trauma.[11] The Pagis poem, "The Tower," and the Borowski story, "World of Stone," both of which I discuss in chapter 3, are especially interesting because each is so literal a description of this breakdown. The Pagis poem tells the story of a small, wordless draft that attempts to make its way up the tower and to the sky but falls apart as does the containing structure of the tower. "World of Stone" traces the repeated birth and collapse of images that form in the writer's mind as he walks through bustling streets to his apartment, where he will sit down and attempt to put his Auschwitz experiences into words. The Pagis poem, like the Borowski story, is about language and the way that extreme experience forecloses the possibility of an "exchange between language and experience." Both leave the "hole" intact and substitute, for the traumatic narrative that cannot be told, the story of the difficulty and, indeed, impossibility of telling such a story. Such strategies and devices are typical of narratives of historical horror.

"Where to begin?" Pagis asks in his poem, "Footprints." He answers, enigmatically and thoughtfully, "very diligent, I immerse myself/ in the laws of heavenly grammar: I am learning/ the declensions and ascensions of/ silence."[12] The silence of which Pagis writes is not a metaphorical silence, and I take his reference to a *grammar* of silence to be literal as well. I close this chapter and the writing of this book in the spirit of Pagis. There is a grammar to learn. There is a grammar to write. These narratives of historical horror and trauma cross a terrible boundary in representation. They are the fabric with the bullet hole at the center. Our literary vocabularies are vocabularies about the familiar staples of experience. We need more accurate formal description and study of narratives on this other side of representational limit, of those stories that cross a boundary and tell the catastrophic and shared experience that is, in its awful way, both unfamiliar and all too familiar.

Notes

Notes to Introduction

1. Jean-François Lyotard, *The Differend: Phrases in Dispute*, Georges Van Den Abbeele (Minneapolis: University of Minnesota, 1988) 13.

Notes to Chapter 1

1. The unrepresentability of the Holocaust is a key theme of all writing on the subject, from the first diary entries in the ghettos to the outpouring of memoirs and of literary and historical writing that has surfaced over the past twenty-five years. With the publication of Jean-François Lyotard's *The Differend* (Minneapolis: University of Minnesota Press, 1988) and the discussion in that work of language and the problematic of testimony, the issue has received scrutiny in detailed theoretical terms. Hayden White, Jacques Derrida, Geoffrey Hartman, and Dennis Donoghue focused on this issue at a conference put together by Saul Friedlander to address this question ("The Limits of Representation," University of California, L.A., April 26–29, 1990). Many of the papers presented appeared in Friedlander's collection of essays, *Probing the Limits of Representation: Nazism and the "Final Solution"* (Cambridge, Massachusetts: Harvard University Press, 1992). Hartman's keynote address appears in this volume as well as in his book: *The Longest Shadow: In the Aftermath of the Holocaust* (Bloomington: Indiana University Press, 1996) under the title "The Book of Destruction."

2. Alvin Rosenfeld, Sidra Ezrahi, and others have insisted upon a distinction between conventional tales of horror and Holocaust literature, a distinction that seems obvious enough. Rosenfeld raises this problem in *A Double Dying: Reflections on Holocaust Literature* (Bloomington: Indiana University Press, 1980). In his opening chapter he discusses the ways we read Poe, Kafka, and even de Sade and the difference between such readings and that of a Holocaust narrative: "the point is that we lack a means of reading Holocaust literature. It has no symbolic dimensions, carries no allegorical weight, possesses no apparent or covert meaning . . ." (22–25).

See also Sidra DeKoven Ezrahi, *By Words Alone: The Holocaust in Literature* (London: University of Chicago Press, 1980) 51 and Lawrence Langer, *The Holocaust and the Literary Imagination* (New Haven: Yale University Press, 1975) 22.

3. Richard Wilbur, "Poe and the Art of Suggestion," *Studies in English*, 3, 1982: 1–13.

4. See the Norton Critical edition of Heart of Darkness: *An Authoritative Text, Backgrounds, Sources, Criticism*, 2nd edition, ed. Robert Kimbrough (New York: Norton, 1971) 160. All citations from this work refer to this edition. Page numbers have been indicated parenthetically in the body of my text.

5. Richard Davis, a well-known journalist of the period, wrote:

> After one has talked with men and women who have seen the atrocities, has seen in the official reports that those accused of the atrocities do not deny having committed them, but point out that they were merely obeying orders, and after one has seen that even at the capital of Boma all the conditions of slavery exist, one is assured that in the jungle, away from the sight of men, all things are possible. . . .   (Kimbrough, 92–93)

6. Ian Watt, *Conrad in the Nineteenth Century* (Berkeley and Los Angeles: University of California Press, 1979) 126–253.

7. Adam Hochschild, *King Leopold's Ghost* (New York: Houghton Mifflin, 1998) 143. See Hochschild's discussion of historical detail as it appears in Conrad's text, 142–49.

8. Milan Kundera, "An Introduction to a Variation," *New York Times Book Review*, Jan. 6, 1985: 1, 26.

9. Kundera's unconventional view of Dostoevsky grows out of the harsh experiences of Nazism and communism. See his novel *Life is Elsewhere* for his moral critique of aesthetic positions based on a Dostoevskian nineteenth-century valorization of feeling and of the self.

10. Edgar Allan Poe, "Metzengerstein," *Selected Writings of Edgar Allen Poe*, ed. Edward H. Davidson (Boston: Houghton Mifflin, 1956) 61–69. All citations from this work refer to this edition. Page references have been indicated parenthetically in the body of my text.

11. By "historical reality" I mean the impression of factuality created when authentic detail of the physical, social, and psychological world enter a work of art. See Patrick Brady, "Fact and Factuality in Literature," *Directions in Literary Criticism: Contemporary Approaches to Literature*, ed. Stanley Weintraub and Phillip Young (University Park, Pennsylvania: Pennsylvania State University, 1973).

By "invented world of romance" I am suggesting a continuum among the pastoral, the fairy tale, and the gothic in which all share an invented character but differ in the emphasis upon an ideal or monstrous version of that invented world or some fantastic mixture of the two. All three are consistent in their reliance upon a narrative principle of disengagement from the observed world.

12. T. S. Eliot, "Hamlet and His Problems," *The Great Critics: An Anthology of Literary Criticism*, ed. Smith and Parks (New York: Norton and Co., 1967) 711.

13. Edgar Allan Poe, "The Philosophy of Composition," *Selected Writings of Edgar Allan Poe*, ed. Edward H. Davidson (Boston: Houghton Mifflin, 1956) 480–491.

14. Hannah Arendt, *The Origins of Totalitarianism* (New York: Meridian Books, 1958) 185. See chapter 7, "Race and Bureaucracy," in which Arendt cites Conrad repeatedly in her historical analysis of European imperialism on the African subcontinent.

15. See Arendt 185 and Hochschild 3, 233. Hochschild, basing himself on population counts done in 1924, estimates the loss of life during Leopold's rule at ten million. Arendt's estimate is considerably higher at twenty to forty million.

16. See Cathy Caruth's *Unclaimed Experience: Trauma, Narrative and History* (Baltimore: Johns Hopkins University Press, 1996) and her collection of essays entitled *Trauma: Explorations in Memory* (Baltimore: Johns Hopkins University Press, 1995).

17. I am grateful to J. Hillis Miller for sharing his unpublished manuscript with me. His notion of a "proliferating relay of witnesses" was especially helpful (*"Heart of Darkness*: Parable and Apocalypse," 12). This paper appeared as *"Heart of Darkness* Revisited" in *Heart of Darkness: Joseph Conrad—A Case Study in Contemporary Criticism*, ed. Ross C. Murfin (New York: St. Martin's Press, 1989) 209–225.

Notes to Chapter 2

1. Aharon Appelfeld, *Badenheim 1939*, trans. Dalya Bilu (New York: Washington Square Press, 1980). Page references to this edition appear parenthetically in the body of my essay. For a view of Appelfeld within a spectrum of Hebrew writings, see Alan Mintz, *Hurban: Responses to Catastrophe in Hebrew Literature* (New York: Columbia University Press, 1984) 203–238. My article "Aharon Appelfeld: A Study of an Image" in *Remembering for the Future*, ed. Yehudah Bauer (New York: Elsevier Science, 1989) examines Appelfeld's writing in a European literary context.

2. There is, by now, a large critical literature on the theme of silence in Holocaust writing. One of the most original and persuasive discussions is Alvin Rosenfeld's "The Poetics of Expiration," which first appeared in the *American Poetry Review* and was later incorporated into chapter 4 of Rosenfeld's *A Double Dying: Reflections of Holocaust Literature* (Bloomington and London: Indiana University Press, 1980).

3. Robert J. Lifton, *The Broken Connection: On Death and Continuity of Life* (New York: Simon and Schuster, 1979) 175.

4. Susan Shapiro, "Towards a Post-Holocaust Hermeneutics of Testimony" 12, unpublished manuscript presented at the University of Minnesota at a conference, "The Impact of the Holocaust on the Humanities," March 1989.

5. Gisele Brelet, "Music and Silence," *Reflections on Art: A Source Book of Writings by Artists, Critics, and Philosophers*, ed. Suzanne K. Langer (New York: Oxford University Press, 1958) 103–121. References to this essay refer to this edition and are indicated parenthetically in the body of my text.

Notes to Chapter 3

1. Bernard P. Dauenhauer, *Silence, the Phenomenon and Its Ontological Significance* (Bloomington, Indiana: Indiana University Press, 1980) 119.

2. Rainer Maria Rilke, *The Selected Poetry of Rainer Maria Rilke*, ed. and trans. Stephen Mitchell (New York: Random House, 1982) 153.

3. Rilke, p. 155. For a discussion of the relevance of Rilke's notion of death after Auschwitz, see the first chapter of Edith Wyschogrod's *Spirit in Ashes: Hegel, Heidegger, and Man-Made Mass Death* (New Haven and London: Yale University Press, 1985).

4. Suzanne Langer, ed., *Reflections on Art: A Source Book of Writings by Artists, Critics, and Philosophers* (Oxford, England: Oxford University Press, 1958) 120–121. Further page references to this article are given in the body of the text.

5. Cited in Dauenhauer, 135.

6. George Steiner, *Language and Silence: Essays on Language, Literature, and the Inhuman* (New York: Atheneum, 1967) 39.

7. Cited by Robert Alter in his discussion of the political and spiritual context out of which Broch wrote his novel. See Alter's *Defenses of the Imagination: Jewish Writers and Modern Historical Crisis* (Philadelphia: Jewish Publication Society, 1977) 9.

8. Dauenhauer, 135.

9. Joseph Chiari, *Symbolisme from Poe to Mallarmé: The Growth of a Myth* (London: Rockliff, 1956) 142.

10. Trans. mine, from the original French cited in Chiari:

Je dis: une fleur, et hors de l'oubli où ma voix relègue aucun contour, entant que quelque d'autre que les calices sus, musicalement se lève, idée même et auve, l'absente de tous bouquets.   (142)

11. Wallace Stevens, *The Collected Poems* (New York: Alfred A. Knopf, 1971). In "The Man with the Blue Guitar," Stevens writes: "It must be this rhapsody or none,/ The rhapsody of things as they are" (183). Further citations from Stevens's poems are all from this edition, and page references appear parenthetically in my text.

12. Cited in Steiner, 52. The citation in its entirety reads:

It is as if, through becoming involved in literature, I had used up all possible symbols without really penetrating their meaning. They no longer have any vital significance for me. Words have killed images or are concealing them. A civilization of words is a civilization distraught. Words create confusion. Words are not the word (les mots ne sont pas la parole). . . . The fact is that words say nothing, if I may put it that way. . . . There are no words for the deepest experience. The more I try to explain myself, the less I understand myself. Of course, not everything is unsayable in words, only the living truth.

13. Samuel Beckett, *Watt, The Norton Anthology of World Masterpieces*, 2 (New York: Norton and Company, 1985) 1924.

14. Jean Améry, *At the Mind's Limit*, trans. Sidney Rosenfeld and Stella P. Rosenfeld (Bloomington: Indiana University Press, 1980) 100.

15. See the text to Claude Lanzmann's film, *Shoah: An Oral History of the Holocaust* (New York: Pantheon Books, 1985). Page references to this text are given in the body of my text.

16. This assertion of the impossibility of description is repeated in every eyewitness account, in every diary, memoir, oral history, and video testimony. It is a central theme of the poetry and fiction of the Holocaust. It is a problem discussed by every literary critic from Adorno onward, and is a key issue in philosophical debate on the question of testimony and its interpretation (see Susan Shapiro's discussion of Fackenheim, Ricoeur and Lyotard, "Towards a Post-Holocaust Hermeneutics of Testimony," presented at the University of Minnesota, at a conference entitled "The Impact of the Holocaust on the Humanities" (December, 1988).

17. In "Writing and the Holocaust," Irving Howe cites Lanzmann:

The destruction of Europe's Jews cannot be logically deduced from any . . . system of presuppositions. . . . Between the conditions that permitted extermination and the extermination itself—the fact of the extermination—there is a break in continuity, a hiatus, an abyss.

See *Writing and the Holocaust*, ed. Beryl Lang (London: Holms and Meier, 1988) 178.

18. See Tony Brinkley and Steven Joura's analysis of this film and of the notion of witnessing in "Tracing Shoah," PMLA III, 1 (1996) 108–127. The paper juxtaposes Peirce's idea of the "index" with Levinas's ethics of otherness in a persuasive view of witnessing as a dimension of language.

19. Particular thanks to J. Hillis Miller for permitting me to examine his article "*Heart of Darkness*: Parable and Apocalypse," prior to its publication. In that essay, Miller emphasizes the "proliferating relay of witnesses" in *Heart of Darkness* (ms., 12).

Miller's essay has since appeared in *Heart of Darkness: A Case Study in Contemporary Criticism*, ed. Ross C. Murfin (New York: St. Martin's Press, 1989.

20. Conrad's juxtaposition of the words "voice" and "word" is fascinating. Insofar as Kurtz is a voice, he embodies a truth of experience that Marlow seeks. On the other hand, Marlow lies to the Intended after she begs to know his dying words: "'His words at least, have not died.'" Kurtz incorporates these conflicting dimensions of language. Hence Marlow refers to Kurtz's: "gift of expression, the bewildering, the illuminating, the most exalted and the most contemptible, the pulsating

stream of light, or the deceitful flow from the heart of darkness" (48).

21. Dan Pagis, *Points of Departure*, trans. Steven Mitchell (Philadelphia: Jewish Publication Society, 1981) 89. Page references to other poems by Pagis refer to this edition and are included in the body of my text. See Sidra Ezrahi's discussion of Pagis's poetry, "Dan Pagis: The Holocaust and the Poetics of Incoherence," *Remembering for the Future*, ed. Yehudah Bauer (New York: Elsevier Science, 1989).

22. "Music and Silence," *Reflections on Art: A Source Book of Writings by Artists, Critics, and Philosophers*, ed. Suzanne Langer (London: Oxford University Press, 1958) 120.

23. Cited in Alan Udoff, "On Poetic Dwelling: Situating Celan and the Holocaust," *Argumentum e Silentio: International Paul Celan Symposium*, ed. Amy Colin (Berlin: Walter de Gruyter, 1987) 349.

24. Cited in Alvin Rosenfeld, *A Double Dying: Reflections on Holocaust Literature* (Bloomington and London: Indiana University Press, 1980) 89.

25. See Frieda Aaron, "Poetry and Ideology in Extremis: Ghetto and Concentration Camp Poetry," *Comparative Poetics: Proceedings of the Xth Congress of the International Association of Comparative Literature*, ed. Claudio Guillen and Peggy Asher (New York: Garland Publishing, 1985) 364.

26. Rosenfeld, 105.

27. Roland Barthes, *Image, Music, Text*, trans. Stephen Heath (New York: Hill and Wang, 1977) 184.

28. For a very nuanced examination of the ways in which voice operates in a literary text, see also Herman Rapaport, "Geoffrey Hartman and the Spell of Sounds," *Rhetoric and Form: Deconstruction at Yale*, ed. Robert Davis and Ronald Schleifer (Norman: University of Oklahoma Press, 1985) 159–177.

29. François Mauriac, in his Foreword to Elie Wiesel's *Night*, ponders the extraordinary impression his wife's voice made upon him:

> I confided to my young visitor that nothing I had seen during those somber years had left so deep a mark upon me as those trainloads of Jewish children standing at Austerlitz station. Yet I did not even see them myself! My wife described them to me, her voice still filled with horror. . . .

Night, trans. Stella Rodway (New York: Hill and Wang, 1960) 7.

30. See Rosenfeld's important discussion of voice and silence in the poetry of Paul Celan, in chapter 4, "Poetics of Expiration," *A Double Dying* (London: Indiana University Press, 1980) 82–90.

31. Stephen Spender, introduction, *Abba Kovner and Nelly Sachs: Selected Poems* (Harmondsworth, England: Penguin Books, 1971) 15.

32. Carolyn Forché, *The Angel of History* (New York: Harper and Row, 1994). Parts of this work appeared in the *Graham House Review*, Colgate University Press, Spring 1988; also, under the title "The Recording Angel," in *Antaeus*, 20th Anniversary issue.

33. Charles Reznikoff, *Holocaust* (Los Angelas: Black Sparrow Press, 1975). See Robert Alter's discussion of Reznikoff, "Charles Reznikoff: Between Present and Past" in *Defenses of the Imagination: Jewish Writers and Historical Crisis* (Philadelphia: Jewish Publication Society, 1977).

34. Charlotte Delbo, *Auschwitz and After*, trans. Rosette C. Lamont (New Haven: Yale University Press, 1995).

35. Shapiro, 13. See note 16.

36. André Schwarz-Bart, *The Last of the Just*, trans. Stephen Becker (New York: Atheneum, 1960). Further page references to this work are included in parenthesis in the body of this text.

37. For a detailed consideration of the connections between voice and physical pain, see Elaine Scarry, *The Body in Pain: The Making and Unmaking of the World* (New York: Oxford University Press, 1985).

38. Shapiro, 14.

39. Jerzy Kosinksi, *The Painted Bird*, 2nd ed. (Boston: Houghton Mifflin, 1976). Further page references to this work are included in parentheses in the body of this text.

40. For a consideration of the condition of muteness in Kosinski's novel, see Sarah Horowitz, *Voicing the Void: Muteness and Memory in Holocaust Fiction* (New York: State University of New York Press, 1997) 71–94. See also Lawrence Langer's discussion of Kosinski in *The Holocaust and the Literary Imagination* (New Haven: Yale University Press, 1975) 166–191.

41. Tadeusz Borowski, *This Way for the Gas, Ladies and Gentlemen*, intro. by Jan Kott, selected and trans. Barbara Vedder (New York: Penguin Books, 1976). Further page references to this work are included in parentheses in the body of my text.

42. Paul Celan, "With a Variable Key," in *Poems of Paul Celan*, trans. Michael Hamburger (New York: Persea Books, 1991) 91.

43. Stevens, 9.

Notes to Chapter 4

1. Cited in Alvin Rosenfeld, *A Double Dying: Reflections on Holocaust Literature* (Bloomington and London: Indiana University Press, 1980) 28.

2. Charlotte Delbo, *None of Us Shall Return*, trans. John Githens (Boston: Beacon Press, 1978) 128.

3. Piotr Rawicz, *Blood from the Sky*, trans. Peter Wiles (New York: Harcourt, Brace & World, 1964).

4. Elie Wiesel, *Night*, foreword by François Mauriac, trans. Stella Rodway (New York: Hill and Wang, 1958). All citations from this work refer to this edition, and page references are included in the body of the article. An earlier version of this chapter appeared in *Elie Wiesel: Between Memory and Hope*, ed. Carol Rittner, R.S.M. (New York: New York University Press, 1990) 120–129.

5. Rolf Krause, "Truth But Not Art? German Autobiographical Writings of the Survivors of Nazi Concentration Camps, Ghettos and Prisons," *Remembering for the Future: The Impact of the Holocaust and Genocide on Jews and Christians*, ed. Yehudah Bauer (New York: Elsevier Science, 1989).

6. Krause, 15. See Lawrence Langer's "Interpreting Survivor Testimony" for an important discussion of the ways in which interviewers mishear, misconstruct and misrepresent survivor testimony in the very process of interviewing survivors. Langer's article is an examination of a problematics of reception based on his work in the Yale Video Archives. The article appeared in an important volume exploring this and related issues of representing "historical horror" entitled *Writing and the Holocaust*, ed. Beryl Lang (New York: Holmes and Meier, 1988) 26–40.

See also Geoffrey H. Hartman, "Testimony, Preserving the Personal Story: The Role of Video Documentation," *Dimensions: A Journal of Holocaust Studies* 1.1 (Spring 1985).

7. For an excellent discussion of language and violent fact, see Frederick Hoffman, *The Mortal No: The Theme of Death in Modern Literature* (Princeton: Princeton University Press, 1964). See chapter 4, "The Moment of Violence: Ernst Juenger and the Literary Problem of Fact," 158–178.

8. Hans Robert Jauss, *Toward an Aesthetic of Reception*, trans. Timothy Bahti (Minneapolis: University of Minnesota Press, 1982) 40.

9. One of the earliest and most important discussions of the issue of psychic trauma and the concentration camp experience from a psychoanalytic perspective is Robert J. Lifton's *The Broken Connection: On Death and the Continuity of Life* (New York: Simon and Schuster, 1979). See especially chapter 13, "Survivor Experience and Traumatic Syndrome," 163–187. See also *Knowing and Not Knowing the Holocaust*, ed. by Dori Laub, M.D. and Nanette C. Auerhahn, *Psychoanalytic Inquiry*:

A Topical Journal for Mental Health Professionals 5.1 (1985), which offers a series of papers devoted to the specific analysis of the problem of reception or "knowing" from a psychiatric point of view as it pertains to the Holocaust. An entire field, trauma studies, has emerged in the last few years spanning literatures in psychiatry (e.g., Bessel van der Kolk), in philosophy (e.g., Herman Rappaport), in literary studies (e.g., Cathy Caruth), and the social sciences (e.g., Arthur Kleinman, Veena Das, and Margaret Lock). An important address was given by Saul Friedlander on the strange ways that resistances to "knowing" the Holocaust makes itself felt in the worlds of artistic and intellectual production at the International Scholars' Conference held in Oxford, England, 10–13 July 1988 entitled, "On the Representation of the *Shoah* in Present-Day Western Culture."

10. Taduesz Borowski similarly describes a splitting of the mind and body in experiencing the horrific knowledge of the crematoria in a short story entitled "The People Who Walked On":

> I stared into the night, numb, speechless, frozen with horror. My entire body trembled and rebelled, somehow even without my participation. I no longer controlled my body, although I could feel its every tremor. My mind was completely calm, only the body seemed to revolt.

The story is from a small volume of Borowski's stories selected and translated from the Polish by Barbara Vedder entitled *This Way for the Gas, Ladies and Gentlemen* (New York: Penguin Books, 1976) 85.

11. As cited in Susan Shapiro, "Towards a Post-Holocaust Hermeneutics of Testimony" 12, unpublished manuscript presented at the University of Minnesota at a conference, "The Impact of the Holocaust on the Humanities," March 1989.

12. See David Roskies's discussion of the "testimonial imperative" in "The Holocaust According to the Literary Critics," *Prooftexts: A Journal of Jewish Literary History* 1.2 (May 1981). Also see Sidra DeKoven Ezrahi's discussion of the same impulse in chapter 2 of *By Words Alone: The Holocaust in Literature* (Chicago and London: University of Chicago Press, 1980).

13. Shapiro.

14. See Lawrence Langer's *Versions of Survival: The Holocaust and the Human Spirit* (Albany: State University of New York Press, 1982); also James E. Young, *Writing and Rewriting the Holocaust: Narrative and the Consequences of Interpretation* (Bloomington and Indianapolis: Indiana University Press, 1988).

Notes to Chapter 5

1. Joseph Conrad, *Heart of Darkness*, ed. Robert Kimbrough (New York: W. W. Norton and Co., 1963) 36.

2. Elie Wiesel, *Night*, trans. Stella Rodway. (New York: Hill and Wang, 1958) 27.

3. Robert J. Lifton, *The Broken Connection: On Death and the Continuity of Life* (New York: Simon and Schuster, 1980) 175. Further citations from this text refer to this edition, and page references are given parenthetically in the body of my text.

4. Primo Levi, "Beyond Survival," *Prooftexts: A Journal of Jewish Literary History*, 4.1 (Jan. 1984): 12,13. The citation reads in full:

> During my imprisonment, despite the hunger, the cold, the blows, the fatigue, the gradual death of my companions, the promiscuity of all hours, I experienced an intense need to recount how much I was living. I knew that my hopes of being saved were minimal, but I also knew that if I survived, I would have to tell the story. I would not be able to do less. To tell the story, to bear witness, was an end for which to save oneself. Not to live and to tell but to live in order to tell.

5. Piotr Rawicz, *Blood from the Sky*, trans. Peter Wiles (New York: Harcourt, Brace & World, 1964); Charlotte Delbo, *None of Us Shall Return*, trans. John Githens (Boston: Beacon Press, 1968). All citations to these works are from these editions and appear parenthetically in the body of my text.

6. The trilogy has been recently translated in its entirety by Rosette C. Lamont under the title: *Auschwitz and After* (New Haven: Yale University Press, 1995).

7. Jean-François Lyotard, *The Differend: Phrases in Dispute*, trans. Georges Van Den Abbeele (Minneapolis: University of Minnesota Press, 1988) 13.

8. Frederick Hoffman, *The Mortal No* (Princeton: Princeton University Press, 1964) 159.

9. Lifton 175. See Lifton's discussion of the "traumatic syndrome," 173–177.

10. Hoffman, 159.

11. Charlotte Delbo, *None of Us Shall Return*, trans. John Githens (Boston: Beacon, 1968). All citations from Delbo's text refer to this edition. Page reference is indicated parenthetically in the body of my text. Parts of this chapter appeared under the title "Art and Testimony: The Represen-

tation of Historical Horror in Literary Works by Piotr Rawicz and Charlotte Delbo," *Cardozo Studies in Law and Literature* 3.2 (Fall 1991) 243–259. Delbo has been insufficiently appreciated in this country. Rosette C. Lamont has written extensively on Delbo and translated her trilogy, *Auschwitz and After* (see note 6), and a posthumous work, *Days and Memory* (Vermont: Marlborough Press, 1990). Lamont's essays on Delbo include "Charlotte Delbo's Frozen Friezes," in *L'esprit Créateur* 19.2 (Spring 1972): 65–74; "Charlotte Delbo: A Woman/Book," which appeared in a volume of essays edited by Alice Kessler-Harris and William McBrien entitled *Faith of a (Woman) Writer* (New York: Greenwood Press, 1988); and "Literature, the Exile's Agent of Survival: Alexander Solzhenitsyn and Charlotte Delbo," which appeared in *Mosaic* 9.1 (1975): 1–17.

Short stories translated by Lamont include "The Gypsy," *Centerpoint: A Journal of Interdisciplinary Studies* 4.1 (Fall 1980): 47–52; "Phantoms, My Companions," *Massachusetts Review* 12 (1971): 10–30; and "Phantoms, My Faithful Ones," *Massachusetts Review* 14 (1973): 310–315.

See also Lawrence Langer, "Charlotte Delbo and a Heart of Ashes," *The Age of Atrocity: Death in Modern Literature* (Boston: Beacon Press, 1978) 201–244.

12. Victor Shklovsky, cited in Richard Weisberg, "Avoiding Central Realities," *Human Rights Quarterly* 5.2 (1983) 153.

13. Jean Amery, *At the Mind's Limit: Contemplations by a Survivor on Auschwitz and Its Realities*, trans. Sidney Rosenfeld and Stella P. Rosenfeld (Bloomington: Indiana University Press, 1980) 33.

14. Hoffman, 174.

15. Czeslaw Milosz, *The Witness of Poetry* (Cambridge, Mass. and London: Harvard University Press, 1983) 56, 57.

Notes to Chapter 6

1. Bessel van der Kolk, "Social and Biological Dimensions of the Compulsion to Forget and Repeat Trauma," lecture at the New School for Social Research, November 21, 1997. The lecture was part of a series entitled "More than Mind Can Endure: Trauma in the Late Twentieth Century."

2. See also chapter 1 in Judith Herman's *Trauma and Recovery: The Aftermath of Violence* (New York: Basic Books, 1992) for a lucid, judicious, and brilliant history of the notion of trauma from the 1880's up to the present day. Herman underlines the crucial presence and role of a validating political movement for each period during which trauma emerges as a focus and subject of study:

To hold traumatic reality in consciousness requires a social context that affirms and protects the victim and that joins victim and witness in a common alliance. For the individual victim, this social context is created by relationships with friends, lovers, and family. For the larger society, the social context is created by political movements that give voice to the disempowered.

The systematic study of psychological trauma therefore depends on the support of a political movement. . . . The study of war trauma becomes legitimate only in a context that challenges the sacrifice of young men in war. . . . Advances in the field occur only when they are supported by a political movement powerful enough to legitimate an alliance between investigators and patients and to counteract the ordinary social processes of silencing and denial.   (Herman 9)

3. Herman, 9.

4. Robert J. Lifton, *The Broken Connection: On Death and Continuity of Life* (New York: Simon and Schuster, 1979). See Cathy Caruth, ed. *Trauma: Explorations in Memory* (Baltimore: Johns Hopkins University Press, 1995) and also by Caruth, *Unclaimed Experience: Trauma, Narrative, History* (Baltimore: Johns Hopkins University Press, 1996).

5. Adam Hochschild, *King Leopold's Ghost* (New York: Houghton Mifflin, 1998).

6. Hochschild, "Mr. Kurtz, I Presume: Possible Prototypes for Literary Villain in J. Conrad's 'Heart of Darkness,'" *The New Yorker* 73:8 (April 14, 1997) 40–47.

7. Terrence Des Pres, *The Survivor: An Anatomy of Life in the Death Camps* (New York: Oxford University Press, 1976) 5.

8. Frederick Hoffman, *The Mortal No: Death and the Modern Imagination* (Princeton: Princeton University Press, 1964) 158–60, 162.

9. Robert Brinkley and Stephen Joura, PMLA 111 (1996) 1:108–127. Page references to citations from this article are included parenthetically in the body of my text. In the context of my discussion in this chapter, it is noteworthy that the introductory essay to this issue of PMLA refers to the Brinkley and Joura article briefly and as "moving," and utterly fails to take note of the carefully laid out and explicit ways that Brinkley and Joura use *Shoah* to address important theoretical questions.

10. Whereas my discussion here and throughout this book is concerned with showing how witnessing comes about precisely when and

where there is a breakdown of the representational function of language, Brinkley and Joura discuss witnessing and the experience of *Shoah* from a Levinasian standpoint:

> In this context, Levinas's understanding of obligation may accurately characterize the experience of viewing the film, the coming-into-being in the second person that constitutes an obligation. By virtue of being addressed, the witness exists as *you*. Interpretation produces an account, what *I* have to say: but witnesses are obliged by their responsibility to that which addresses them: the sign and its referent; voices, settings, and the film; other witnesses and the Shoah those witnesses index. Witnesses are obliged not to replace these things with what *they* have to say. . . .   (126)

11. Chapter 3 examines a series of works within which this "disruption" of the "exchange between language and experience" occurs. In that chapter I sometimes refer to the representing of distinct domains of language and of experience that have lost connection to one another and that function as a sign of trauma. Interestingly enough, the van der Kolk lecture (see note 1 above) included a fairly technical discussion of the biological and physiological changes at the brain level that occur with trauma. These include changes in the usual routes of communication between language and emotional sites in the brain. Van der Kolk's clinical and medical descriptions of trauma parallel, in unexpected and startling ways, my own observations of specific literary works of historical horror, their shapes and stylistic features.

One might speculate that texts that employ certain narrative and rhetorical designs in representing historical horror replicate artistically a biology of trauma.

12. Dan Pagis, *Points of Departure*, trans. Stephen Mitchell (Philadelphia: Jewish Publication Society, 1981) 29–37.

Works Consulted

Aichinger, Ilse. *Herod's Children*. Trans. Cornelia Schaeffer. New York: Atheneum Press, 1963.

Alexander, Edward. *The Resonance of Dust: Essays on Holocaust Literature and Jewish Fate*. Columbus: Ohio State University Press, 1979.

Alter, Robert. *Defenses of the Imagination: Jewish Writers and Modern Historical Crisis*. Philadelphia: Jewish Publication Society, 1977.

——. "Jewish Humor and the Domestication of Myth." *Veins of Humor*. Ed. Harry Levin. Harvard English Studies No. 3. Cambridge, Mass.: Harvard University Press, 1972.

——. "Psychological and Moral Dilemmas," *New York Times Magazine* May 15, 1983.

——. *After the Tradition*. New York: Dutton, 1969.

Alvarez, Alfred. *Beyond All This Fiddle*. New York: Random House, 1969. See also *Commentary*, Nov. 1964: 65–69.

——. "The Literature of the Holocaust." *Commentary*, Nov. 1964: 65–69.

Améry, Jean. *At the Mind's Limit: Contemplations by a Survivor on Auschwitz and Its Realities*. Trans. Sidney Rosenfeld and Stella P. Rosenfeld. Bloomington: Indiana University Press, 1980.

Appelfeld, Aharon. *The Age of Wonders*. Trans. Dalya Bilu. Boston: David R. Godine, 1981.

——. *Badenheim 1939*. Trans. Dalya Bilu. New York: Washington Square Press, 1980.

——. "Kitty." *Modern Hebrew Stories*. Ed. E. Spicehandler. New York: Bantam, 1971.

———. *The Immortal Bartfuss.* New York: Wiedenfeld and Nicolson, 1988.

———. *To the Land of the Cattails.* Trans. Jeffrey Green. New York: Wiedenfeld and Nicolson, 1986.

———. *The Retreat.* Trans. Dalya Bilu. New York: Viking Penguin, Inc., 1985.

———. *Tzili: The Story of a Life.* Trans. Dalya Bilu. New York: E.P. Dutton, Inc., 1983.

Arendt, Hannah. *Eichmann in Jerusalem: A Report on the Banality of Evil.* New York: Viking Press, 1965.

———. *The Origins of Totalitarianism.* Cleveland and New York: World Publishing Co., 1985.

Aron, Frieda. *Bearing the Unbearable: Yiddish and Polish Poetry in the Ghettos and Concentration Camps.* Albany: State University of New York Press, 1990.

———. "Poetry and Ideology in Extremis: Ghetto and Concentration Camp Poetry." *Comparative Poetics: Proceedings of the Xth Congress of the International Comparative Literature Association.* Ed. Claudio Guillen and Peggy Asher. New York: Garland Publishing, 1985.

———. "Yiddish and Polish Poetry in the Ghettos and Camps." *Modern Language Studies* 19.1 (Winter 1989): 72–87.

Balakian, Peter. *Black Dog of Fate: An American Son Uncovers His Armenian Past.* New York: Basic Books, 1997.

Baron, Salo W. *From a Historian's Notebook: European Jewry Before and After Hitler.* Preprints from *American Jewish Yearbook* 63 (1962). American Jewish Committee, Institute of Human Relations.

Barthes, Roland. *Image, Music, Text.* Trans. Stephen Heath. New York: Hill and Wang, 1977.

Bellow, Saul. *Mr. Sammler's Planet.* New York: Viking, 1963.

Bentley, Eric, ed. *The Storm Over the Deputy.* New York: Grove Press, Inc., 1964.

Bettleheim, Bruno. *The Informed Heart.* Glencoe, Illinois: Free Press, 1960.

Blanchot, Maurice. *Writing of the Disaster.* Trans. Ann Smock. Lincoln: University of Nebraska Press, 1986.

Bloom, Harold. "Inescapable Poe." *New York Review of Books* 11 Oct. 1984: 23–36.

Bloom, Sandra. *Creating Sanctuary: Toward the Evolution of Sane Societies.* New York: Routledge, 1997.

Borowski, Tadeusz. *This Way for the Gas, Ladies and Gentlemen.* Selected and trans. Barbara Vedder. Intro. Jan Kott. Intro. trans. Michael Kandel. New York: Penguin, 1976.

Bosmajian, Hamida. *Metaphors of Evil: Contemporary German Literature and the Shadow of Nazism*. Iowa City: University of Iowa Press, 1979.

Brady, Frank. "Fact and Factuality in Literature." *Directions in Literary Criticism: Contemporary Approaches to Literature*. Ed. Stanley Weintraub and Phillip Young. University Park: Pennsylvania State University Press, 1973.

Braham, Randolf, ed. *Reflections of the Holocaust in Art and Literature*. New York: Social Science Monographs, Boulder and Csengeri Institute for Holocaust Studies of the Graduate School and University Center of the City of New York, 1990.

Brelet, Giselle. "Music and Silence." *Reflections on Art: A Source Book of Writings by Artists, Writers, and Philosophers*. Ed. Suzanne K. Langer. London: Oxford University Press, 1972.

Brinkley, R. and S. Joura. "Tracing Shoah." *PMLA* III (1996): 108–127.

Brodsky, Joseph. "Uncommon Visage." *Poets and Writers* 16.2 (March/April 1988). 1987 Nobel acceptance speech.

Brombert, Victor. "The Happy Prison: A Recurring Romantic Metaphor." *Romanticism: Vistas, Instances, Continuities*. Ed. David Thorburn and Geoffrey Hartman. Ithaca: Cornell University Press, 1973. 62–79.

Brown, Daniel P., Alan W. Scheflin and D. Corydon Hammond. *Memory, Trauma Treatment, and the Law: An Essential Reference on Memory for Clinicians, Researchers, Attorneys, and Judges*. New York: Norton, 1998.

Calvino, Italo. "The Written and the Unwritten Word." *New York Review of Books* 12 May, 1983.

Cargas, Harry James. *Responses to Elie Wiesel*. New York: Perdia Books, 1978.

Caruth, Cathy, ed. *Trauma: Explorations in Memory*. Baltimore: Johns Hopkins University Press, 1995.

———. *Unclaimed Experience: Trauma, Narrative, and History*. Baltimore: Johns Hopkins University Press, 1996.

Celan, Paul. "With a Variable Key." *Poems of Paul Celan*. Trans. Michael Hamburger. New York: Persea Books, 1999.

Chiari, Joseph. *Symbolism from Poe to Mallarmé: Growth of a Myth*. London: Rockcliff, 1956.

Conrad, Joseph. *Heart of Darkness: An Authoritative Text, Backgrounds and Sources, Criticism*. Ed. Robert Kimbrough. 2nd ed. New York: Norton, 1971.

Czath, Geza. "Little Emma: A Story." *New York Review of Books*, 16 June 1983: 18–20.

Danieli, Yael. "The Treatment and Prevention of Long-Term Effects and Intergenerational Transmission of Victimization: A Lesson from Holocaust Survivors and Their Children." *Trauma and Its Effects*. Ed. Charles R. Figley. New York: Brunner/Mazal, 1985. 296–313.

Dauenhauer, Bernard P. *Silence, the Phenomenon and Its Ontological Significance*. Bloomington: Indiana University Press, 1980.

Dawidowicz, Lucy. *A Holocaust Reader*. New York: Behrman House, Inc., 1976.

———. *The War Against the Jews, 1933–1945*. New York: Holt, Rinehart and Winston, 1975.

———. "What Is the Subject Matter of the Holocaust: A Historian's Perspective." MLA Convention. New York. 27 Dec. 1976.

Delbo, Charlotte. *Auschwitz et Après*. . . . Paris: Les Editions de Minuit, 1970. This title refers to a trilogy of three works by Delbo: *Aucun de Nous Ne Reviendra; Une Connaissance Inutile; Mesure de Nos Jours*.

———. *Auschwitz and After*. Trans. Rosette C. Lamont. New Haven: Yale University Press, 1995.

———. *Le Convoi De 24 Janvier*. Paris: Les Editions de Minuit, 1965.

———. *Days and Memory*. Trans. and ed. Rosette C. Lamont. Marlboro, Vermont: Marlboro Press, 1990.

———. *Qui Rapportera Ces Paroles? Tragedie en Trois Actes*. Paris: P.J. Oswald, 1974.

———. *None of Us Shall Return*. Trans. John Githens. Boston: Beacon Press, 1968.

———. *Spectres, Mes Compagnons*. Lausanne: M. Bridel, 1977.

Demetz, Peter. "The Postwar German Novel, or Starting Over from Scratch." *The German Literary Supplement*. The German Book Fair in New York. March 4–7, 1983.

Des Pres, Terrence. *The Survivor: An Anatomy of Life in the Death Camps*. New York: Oxford University Press, 1976.

———. "Terror and the Sublime." *Human Rights Quarterly*. Special Issue on Terror in the Modern Age (May 1983).

———. "The Dreaming Back." *Centerpoint: A Journal of Interdisciplinary Studies*. 4.1 (Fall 1980). Special issue on the Holocaust.

———. *Writing into the World: Essays 1973–1987*. New York: Viking, 1991.

Efros, Israel, ed. "In the City of Slaughter." *The Complete Poetic Works of Hayyim Nahman Bialik*. New York: Histadruth Ivrith of America, 1948.

Ezrahi, Sidra Dekoven. *By Words Alone: The Holocaust in Literature*. London: University of Chicago Press, 1980.

————. "Dan Pagis: The Holocaust and the Poetics of Incoherence." *Remembering for the Future*. New York: Elsevier Science, 1989.

————. "Revisioning the Past: The Changing Legacy of the Holocaust in Hebrew Literature." *Salmagundi* 68–69 (Fall-Winter 1985–86): 245–270.

Felman, Shoshana and Dori Laub. *Testimony: The Crisis of Witnessing in Literature, Psychoanalysis, and History*. New York: Routledge, 1992.

Felstiner, John. *Paul Celan: Poet, Survivor, Jew*. New Haven: Yale University Press, 1995.

Fine, Ellen S. "The Absent Memory: The Act of Writing in French Holocaust Literature." *Writing and the Holocaust*. Ed. Berel Lang. New York: Holms and Meier, 1988.

————. *Legacy of Night: The Literary Universe of Elie Wiesel*. Foreword. Terrence Des Pres. Albany: State University of New York, 1978.

————. "Literature as Resistance: Survival in the Camps." *Holocaust and Genocide Studies* 1.1 (1986): 79–89.

————. "The Search for Identity: Post-Holocaust French Literature." *Remembering for the Future*. New York: Pergamon Press, 1989.

Fink, Ida. *A Scrap of Time*. Trans. Madeline Levine and Francine Prose. New York: Schocken Books, 1987.

Fleishner, Eva. *Auschwitz: Beginning of a New Era/Reflections on the Holocaust*. New York: Ktav Publishing House, Inc., 1977.

Forché, Carolyn. *Against Forgetting: Twentieth Century Poetry of Witness*. New York: Norton, 1995.

————. *The Angel of History*. New York: Harper and Row, 1994.

Foerster, Norman. "Humanism in the Twentieth Century." *Perspectives in Modern Literature*. Ed. Frederick J. Hoffman. Illinois and New York: Row, Peterson and Co., 1962.

Fraser, John. *Violence in the Arts*. New York: Cambridge University Press, 1974.

Fridman, Lea W. See Hamaoui, Lea.

Friedlander, Albert., ed. *Out of the Whirlwind: A Reader of Holocaust Literature*. New York: Union of American Hebrew Congregations, 1968.

Friedlander, Saul. *Probing the Limits of Representation: Nazism and the Final Solution*. Cambridge: Harvard University Press, 1993.

————. *When Memory Comes*. Trans. Helen R. Lane. New York: Farrar, Straus & Giroux, 1979.

Fromm, Erich. *The Anatomy of Human Destructiveness*. New York: Holt, Rinehart and Winston, Inc. 1975.

Fussel, Paul. *The Great War and Modern Memory*. New York: Oxford University Press, 1975.

Gage, Nicholas. "My Mother Eleni: The Search for Her Executioners." *New York Times Magazine* 3 April 1983.

Gary, Roman. *The Dance of Genghis Cohn.* New York: World Publishing Co., 1968.

Glatstein, Jacob, Samuel Margoshes and Israel Knox, eds. *An Anthology of Holocaust Literature.* Philadelphia: Jewish Publication Society, 1969.

Golz, Sabine. "De- and Relocalization: Strategies of the Poetic Subject in Paul Celan's Early Poetry." Unpublished manuscript of the International Association for Philosophy and Literature. University of Notre Dame, April 1988.

Goodhart, Sandor. *Sacrificing Commentary: Reading the End of Literature.* Baltimore: Johns Hopkins University Press, 1996.

Gourevitch, Philip. *We Wish to Inform You That Tomorrow We Will Be Killed with Our Families: Stories From Rwanda.* New York: Farrar, Straus & Giroux, 1998.

Grass, Günther. *The Tin Drum.* Trans. Ralf Manheim. New York: Vintage Books, 1964.

Grossman, Vasily. *Life and Fate.* Trans. Robert Chandler. New York: Harper and Row, 1985.

Haft, Cynthia. *The Theme of Nazi Camps in French Literature.* The Hague, Paris: Mouton, 1973.

Halperin, Irving. *Messengers From the Dead: Literature of the Holocaust.* Philadelphia: The Westminster Press, 1970.

Hamaoui, Lea (Fridman, Lea W.). "Aharon Appelfeld's *Badenheim 1939*: A Study of an Image." *Remembering for the Future.* Ed. Yehudah Bauer. New York: Elsevier Science, 1989.

———. "Art and Testimony: The Representation of Historical Horror in Literary Works by Piotr Rawicz and Charlotte Delbo." *Cardozo Studies in Law and Literature.* 3.2 (Fall 1991).

———. "Narrative Strategies in the Literature of the Holocaust," *Centerpoint: A Journal of Interdisciplinary Studies* 4.1 (Fall 1980). Special issue on the Holocaust.

———. "The Shape of Night." *Elie Wiesel: Between Memory and Hope.* New York: New York University Press, 1990.

———, Ellen Fine, Jane Gerber and Rosette C. Lamont, eds. *Centerpoint: A Journal of Interdisciplinary Studies* 4.1 (Fall 1980). Special issue on the Holocaust.

Hamburger, Michael. *The Truth of Poetry: Tensions in Modern Poetry From Baudelaire to the 1960's.* London: The Camelot Press, 1965.

———. *From Prophecy to Exorcism: The Premises of Modern German Literature.* London: The Camelot Press, 1965.

Hartman, Geoffrey, ed. *Bitburg in Moral and Political Perspective*. Bloomington: Indiana University Press, 1986.

———, ed. *Holocaust Remembrance: The Shapes of Memory*. Cambridge, Mass: Basil Blackwell, 1994.

———. *The Fateful Question of Culture*. New York: Columbia University Press, 1998.

———. *The Longest Shadow: In the Aftermath of the Holocaust*. Bloomington: Indiana University Press, 1994.

———. "The Weight of What Happened." Rev. of *Zakhor: Jewish History and Jewish Memory* by Joseph Hayim Yerushalmi and of *From a Ruined Garden: The Memorial Books of Polish Jewry* ed. and trans. by Jack Kugelmass and Jonathan Boyarin in *Midstream: A Journal of Jewish Thought*: 30–35.

———. "Testimony: Preserving the Personal Story: The Role of Video Documentation." *Dimensions: A Journal of Holocaust Studies* 1.1 (Spring 1985): 14–18.

Hatley, James. "*Grund* and *Abrund*: Questioning Poetic Fundations in Heidegger and Celan." Annual Meeting of the International Association for Literature and Philosophy, University of Notre Dame, April 1988.

Hay, Malcolm. *The Pressure of Christendom on the People of Israel for 1900 Years*. Boston: Beacon Press, 1961.

Hochschild, Adam. *King Leopold's Ghost*. New York: Houghton Mifflin, 1998.

Hoffman, Frederick. *The Mortal No: Death and the Modern Imagination*. Princeton, New Jersey: Princeton University Press, 1964.

Horowitz, Sarah. *Voicing the Void: Muteness and Memory in Holocaust Fiction*. Albany: State University of New York Press, 1997.

Howe, Irving. "Writing and the Holocaust." *Writing and the Holocaust*. Ed. Beryl Lang. New York: Holmes and Meier, 1988.

———. *Politics and the Novel*. New York: Avon, 1970.

Jameson, Frederic. "Figural Relativism, or the Poetics of Historiography." Rev. of *Metahistory: The Historical Imagination in Nineteenth-Century Europe* by Hayden White. *Diacritics*. Spring 1976.

Jauss, Hans Robert. *Towards an Aesthetics of Reception*. Trans. Timothy Bahti. Minneapolis: University of Minnesota Press, 1982.

Kafka, Franz. *The Complete Stories*. Ed. Nahum N. Glatzer. New York: Schocken Books, 1971.

Kahler, Erich. *The Tower and the Abyss: An Inquiry into the Transformation of Man*. New York: Viking Press, 1957.

Katznelson, Yitzhak. *The Song of the Murdered Jewish People*. Trans. and annotated by Noah Rosenbloom. Israel: Hakibbutz Hameuchad Publishing House, 1980.

Kayser, Wolfgang. *The Grotesque in Art and in Literature.* Trans. Ulrich Weisstein. New York: McGraw Hill, 1966.

King, Robert. "Psychic Numbing in Grumberg's *L'Atelier.*" *The Massachusetts Review* 26.4 (Winter 1985).

Kirchheimer, Manfred. "Beyond the Cliches of the Holocaust: A Filmmaker's View." Paper presented at the Annual Meeting of the International Association for Philosophy and Literature. Special session on "The Aesthetics of the Holocaust." University of Notre Dame, April 21, 1988.

Kleinman, Arthur, Veena Das, Margaret M. Lock and Talal Asad, eds. *Social Suffering.* Berkeley: University of California Press, 1997.

Kosinski, Jerzy. *The Painted Bird.* 2nd ed. Boston: Houghton Mifflin and Co., 1976.

Kovner, Abba and Nelly Sachs. *Selected Poemanuscript* Trans. Shirley Kaufman, Nurit Orchan, Michael Hamburger, Ruth and Mathew Mead and Michael Roloff. Harmondsworth, England: Penguin Books, 1971.

Krause, Rolf D. "Truth but Not Art? German Autobiographical Writings of the Survivors of Nazi Concentration Camps, Ghettos and Prisons." *Remembering for the Future.* New York: Elsevier Science, 1989.

Kristeva, Julia. *Powers of Horror: An Essay on Abjection.* Trans. Leon S. Roudiez. New York: Columbia University Press, 1982.

Kundera, Milan. *Life Is Elsewhere.* Trans. Peter Kursi. New York: Knopf, 1974.

———. *The Unbearable Lightness of Being.* Trans. Michael Henry Heim. New York: Harper and Row, 1984.

———. "A Little History Lesson." *New York Review of Books* 22 Nov. 1984.

———. "The Tragedy of Central Europe." *New York Review of Books.* 26 April 1984: 33–38.

———. "An Introduction to a Variation." *New York Times Book Review.* Jan. 1985: 1, 26.

LaCapra, Dominick. *History and Memory After Auschwitz.* Ithaca: Cornell University Press, 1998.

———. *Representing the Holocaust: History, Theory, Trauma.* Ithaca: Cornell University Press, 1994.

Lamont, Rosette, trans. *Auschwitz and After.* New Haven: Yale University Press, 1995.

———. "Charlotte Delbo: A Woman/Book." *Faith of a (Woman) Writer.* Ed. Alice Kessler Harris and William McBrien. New York: Greenwood Press, 1988. 247–252.

———. "Charlotte Delbo's Frozen Friezes." *L'Esprit Createur* 19.2: 65–74.

———, trans. and foreword. *Days and Memory.* Marlboro, Vermont: Marlboro Press, 1990.

———. "Elie Wiesel: In Search of a Tongue." *Confronting the Holocaust.* Ed. Alvin Rosenfeld and Irving Greenberg. Bloomington: Indiana University Press, 1978.

———. "Literature, the Exile's Agent of Survival: Alexander Solzhenitsyn and Charlotte Delbo." *Mosaic* 9.1 (1975): 1–17.

———, trans. "Phantoms, My Companions." *Massachusetts Review* 12 (1971): 10–30.

———, trans. "Phantoms, My Faithful Ones." *Massachusetts Review* 14 (1973): 310–315.

———. "Samuel Beckett's Wandering Jew." *Reflections of the Holocaust in Literature.* Ed. Randolf Braham. New York: Social Science Monographs, Boulder and the Csengeri Institute for Holocaust Studies of the Graduate School and University Center of the City of New York, 1990. 35–53.

Lang, Berel. *Writing and the Holocaust.* New York and London: Holmes and Meier, 1988.

———. "Writing-the-Holocaust: Jabez and the Measure of History." *The Sin of the Book: Edmond Jabez.* Ed. Eric Gould. Lincoln: University of Nebraska, 1985.

Langer, Lawrence. *The Age of Atrocity: Death in Modern Literature.* Boston: Beacon Press, 1978.

———. "To Express the Inexpressible: The Holocaust Literature of Aharon Appelfeld." *Remembering for the Future.* Ed. Yehudah Bauer. New York: Elsevier Science, 1989.

———. *The Holocaust and the Literary Imagination.* New Haven and London: Yale University Press, 1975.

———. *Holocaust Testimonies: The Ruins of Memory.* New Haven: Yale University Press, 1991

———. "Interpreting Survivor Testimony." *Writing and the Holocaust.* Ed. Berel Lang. New York and London: Holms and Meier, 1988. 26–40.

———. *Versions of Survival: The Holocaust and the Human Spirit.* Albany: State University of New York, 1982.

Langer, Suzanne K., ed. *Reflections on Art: Book of Writings by Artists, Critics, and Philosophers.* London: Oxford University Press, 1972.

Lanzmann, Claude. Shoah: *An Oral History of the Holocaust: The Complete Text of the Film.* Pref. Simone de Beauvoir. New York: Pantheon Books, 1985.

Laub, Dori. "Failed Empathy." *Psychoanalytic Psychology* 6.4: 1989.

—— and Nannette C. Auerhahn, eds. "Knowing and Not Knowing the Holocaust." *Psychoanalytic Inquiry* 5.1: 1985.

Levi, Primo. "Beyond Survival." *Prooftexts* 4.1 (June 1984): 12,13.

——. *The Drowned and the Saved.* Trans. Raymond Rosenthal. New York: Summit Books, 1986.

——. *The Periodic Table.* Trans. Raymond Rosenthal. New York: Schocken Books, 1984.

——. *Survival in Auschwitz.* Trans. Stuart Woolf. New York: Collier, 1969.

Lifton, Robert Jay. *The Broken Connection: On Death and Continuity of Life.* New York: Simon and Schuster, 1979.

Lustig, Arnost. *Indecent Dreamanuscript* Trans. Iris Urwin-Levil, Vera Borkovec and Paul Wilson. Evanston: Illinois University Press, 1968.

Lyotard, Jean-Francois. *The Differend: Phrases in Dispute.* Trans. Georges Van Den Abbeele. Minneapolis: University of Minnesota Press, 1988.

Mailer, Norman. "The White Negro." *Perspectives on Modern Literature.* Ed. Frederick J. Hoffman. Illinois: Row, Peterson and Co., 1982.

Mandel, Siegfried. "In the Wake of Organized Madness." *Contemporary European Novelists.* Ed. Seigfried Mandel. Carbondale: Southern Illinois University Press, 1968.

Migot, Olga Wormser-Migot. *Le System Concentrationnaire Nazi, 1933–45.* Paris: Presses Universitaires de France, 1968.

Miller, J. Hillis. "Heart of Darkness: Parable and Apocalypse." Unpublished manuscript.

——. "Heart of Darkness Revisited," *Heart of Darkness: A Case Study in Contemporary Criticism.* Ed. Ross C. Murfin. New York: St. Martin's Press, 1989.

Milosz, Czeslaw. *The Captive Mind.* Trans. Jane Zielonko. New York: Random House, 1953.

——. *The Witness of Poetry.* Cambridge, Massachusettes: Harvard University Press, 1983.

——. *Selected Poemanuscript* New York: The Ecco Press, 1973.

Mintz, Alan. *Hurban: Responses to Catastrophe in Hebrew Literature.* New York: Columbia University Press, 1984.

Mintz, Ruth Finer, ed. and trans. *Modern Hebrew Poetry: A Bilingual Anthology.* Berkeley and Los Angeles: University of California Press, 1968.

Mitchell, Stephen, ed. and trans. *The Selected Poetry of Rainer Maria Rilke.* New York: Random House, 1982.

Morante, Elsa. *History: A Novel*. Trans. William Weaver. New York: Vintage Books, 1984.

Mosse, George L. *The Crisis of German Ideology: Intellectual Origins of the Third Reich*. New York: Grosset and Dunlop, 1964.

Mulisch, Harry. *The Assault*. Trans. Claire Nicholas White. New York: Pantheon Books, 1985.

Neher, Andre. *The Exile of the Word: From the Silence of the Bible to the Silence of Auschwitz*. Trans. David Maisel. Philadelphia: Jewish Publication Society, 1981.

Nolte, Ernst. *The Three Faces of Fascism*. New York: Mentor Books, 1963.

Otto, Rudolf. *The Idea of the Holy: An Inquiry into the Non-rational Factor in the Idea of the Divine and Its Relation to the Rational*. Trans. John W. Harvey. London: Oxford University Press, 1970.

Ozick, Cynthia. "Rosa." *The Shawl*. New York: Random House, 1980.

———. *The Messiah of Stockholm*. New York: Alfred A. Knopf, 1987.

Pagis, Dan. *Points of Departure*. Trans. Stephen Mitchell. Intro. Robert Alter. Philadelphia: Jewish Publication Society, 1981.

Pasternak, Boris. *Dr. Zhivago*. Trans. May Hayward and Manya Harari. "The Poems of Yurii Zhivago." Trans. Bernard Guilbert Guerny. New York: Pantheon, 1958.

Paulson, Ronald. *Representations of Revolution (1789–1820)*. New Haven and London: Yale University Press, 1983.

Penkower, Monty Noam. *The Jews Were Expendable: Free World Diplomacy and the Holocaust*. Chicago: University of Illinois Press, 1983.

Picard, Max. *The World of Silence*. Trans. Stanley Goodman. Chicago: H. Regnery, 1952.

Poe, Edgar Allan. *The Annotated Tales of Edgar Allan Poe*. Ed. Stephen Peithmen. New York: Doubleday, 1981.

———. "The Philosophy of Composition." *Selected Writings of Edgar Allan Poe*. Ed. Edward H. Davidson. Boston: Houghton Mifflin, 1956.

Ramras-Rauch, Gila and Joseph Michman-Melkman, eds. *Facing the Holocaust: Selected Israeli Fiction*. New York: Jewish Publication Society, 1985.

Rapaport, Herman. *Between the Sign and the Gaze*. Ithaca: Cornell University Press, 1994.

———. "Geoffrey Hartman and the Spell of Sounds." *Rhetoric and Form: Deconstruction at Yale*. Ed. Robert Davis and Ronald Schleifer. Norman: University of Oklahoma Press, 1985. 159–177.

Rawicz, Piotr. *Blood From the Sky*. Trans. Peter Wiles. New York: Harcourt, Brace & World, 1964.

Reznikoff, Charles. *Holocaust*. Los Angeles: Black Sparrow Press, 1975.

Rittner, Carol, ed. *Elie Wiesel: Between Memory and Hope*. New York and London: New York University Press, 1990.

Robbins, Jill. "The Writing of the Holocaust: Claude Lanzmann's *Shoah*." *Prooftexts: A Journal of Jewish Literary History* 7.3 (Sept. 1987): 247–258.

Rosenfeld, Alvin H. *A Double Dying: Reflectons on Holocaust Literature*. Bloomington and London: Indiana University Press, 1980.

———. "The Story of Three Books." *Midstream* (May 1984): 51–54.

——— and Irving Greenberg. *Confronting the Holocaust*. Bloomington: Indiana University Press, 1978.

Roskies, David. *Against the Apocalypse: Responses to Catastrophe in Modern Jewish Culture*. Cambridge, Massachusetts: Harvard University Press, 1984.

———. "Catastrophe in Jewish Literature." *Prooftexts: A Journal of Jewish Literary History* 2.1 (1982).

———. "The Holocaust According to the Literary Critics." *Prooftexts* 1.2 (1981).

Scarry, Elaine. *The Body in Pain: The Making and Unmaking of the World*. New York: Oxford University Press, 1985.

Scholes, Robert and Robert Kellogg. *The Nature of Narrative*. London: Oxford University Press, 1971.

Schulman, Elias. *The Holocaust in Yiddish Literature*. New York: Workman's Circle, 1983.

Schwarz-Bart, André. *The Last of the Just*. Trans. Stephen Becker. New York: Atheneum House, 1960.

Semprun, Jorge. *The Long Voyage*. Trans. Richard Seaver. New York: Grove Press Inc., 1964.

Shapiro, Susan. "Toward a Post-Holocaust Hermeneutics of Testimony." Unpublished manuscript. Presented at University of Minnesota Conference, "Impact of the Holocaust on the Humanities." March 1989.

Siebers, Tobin. "Hannah Arendt's *Eichmann* and the Aesthetics of Storytelling." Unpublished manuscript. Presented at the International Association for Philosophy and Literature. University of Notre Dame. April 1988.

Singer, Isaac Bashevis. *Enemies: A Love Story*. New York: Farrar, Strauss, Giroux, 1972.

Szonyi, David M., ed. *The Holocaust: An Annotated Bibliography and Resource Guide*. New York: Ktav Publishing House, Inc., 1985.

Spender, Steven. Introduction. *Abba Kovner and Nelly Sachs: Selected Poemanuscript* Penguin Modern European Poets. Harmondsworth, England: Penguin Books, 1971.

Spiegelman, Art. *Maus: A Survivor's Tale.* New York: Pantheon Books, 1986.

Steiner, George. *After Babel.* London: Oxford University Press, 1975.

———. *In Bluebeard's Castle.* New Haven: Yale University Press, 1971.

———. *Extraterritoriality: Papers on Literature and the Language Revolution.* New York: Atheneum, 1971.

———. *Language and Silence: Essays on Language, Literature, and the Inhuman.* New York: Atheneum, 1967.

———. "The Long Life of Metaphor: An Approach to 'the Shoah.'" *Writing and the Holocaust.* Ed. Berel Lang. New York: Holms and Meier, 1989.

Stendhal. *The Charterhouse of Parma.* New York: Doubleday, 1956.

Stevens, Wallace. *The Collected Poemanuscript* New York: Alfred A. Knopf, 1971.

Styron, William. *Sophie's Choice.* New York: Random House, 1979.

Syrkin, Marie. "The Literature of the Holocaust." *Midstream: A Monthly Jewish Review* May 1964: 3–20.

Theweleit, Klaus. *Male Fantasies: Women, Floods, Bodies, History.* Trans. Stephen Conway. Minneapolis: University of Minnesota Press, 1987.

Thomas, D. M. "On Literary Celebrity." *New York Times Magazine* 13 June 1982: 24–38.

———. *The White Hotel.* New York: Pocket Books, 1981.

Udoff, Alan. "On Poetic Dwelling: Situating Celan and the Holocaust." *Argumentum e Silentio: International Paul Celan Symposium.* Ed. Amy Colin. Berlin: Walter de Gruyter, 1987.

van der Kolk, Bessel A., Alexander C. McFarlane and Lars Weisaeth, eds. *Traumatic Stress: The Effects of Overwhelming Experience on Mind, Body, and Society.* New York: The Guilford Press, 1996.

Watt, Ian. *Conrad in the Nineteenth Century.* Berkeley and Los Angeles: University of California Press, 1979.

Weisberg, Richard. "Avoiding Central Realities." *Human Rights Quarterly* 5.2 (1983): 153.

———. *The Failure of the Word: The Protagonist as Lawyer in Modern Fiction.* New Haven: Yale University Press, 1984.

———. *Vichy Law and the Holocaust in France.* New York: New York University Press, 1996.

White, Hayden. *Tropics of Discourse: Essays in Cultural Criticism.* Baltimore and London: John Hopkins University Press, 1978.

Wiesel, Elie. *The Accident.* Trans. Anne Borchardt. New York: Avon Books, 1962.

———. *A Beggar in Jerusalem*. New York: Avon, 1971.

———. *Dawn*. Trans. Frances Frenaye. New York: Avon Books, 1961.

———. *The Gates of the Forest*. Trans. F. Frenaye. New York: Avon, 1966.

———. *The Oath*. Trans. Marion Wiesel. New York: Random House, 1973.

———. *The Town beyond the Wall*. Trans. Stephen Becker. New York: Avon Books, 1964.

———. *Night*. Trans. Stella Rodway. New York: Hill and Wang, 1960.

Wyman, David. "Why Auschwitz Was Never Bombed." *Commentary* 65 (May, 1978).

Wyschogrod, Edith. *Spirit in Ashes: Hegel, Heidegger, and Man-Made Mass Death*. New Haven and London: Yale University Press, 1985.

Yerushalmi, Yosef Hayim. *Zakhor: Jewish History and Jewish Memory*. Seattle and London: University of Washington Press, 1982.

Young, James E. "Holocaust Documentary Fiction: Novelist as Eye-Witness." *Writing and the Holocaust*. Ed. Berel Lang. New York: Holms and Meier, 1988.

———. "Interpreting Literary Testimony: A Preface to Rereading Holocaust Diaries and Memoirs." *New Literary History: A Journal of Thought and Interpretation*. 18.2 (Winter 1987): 403–423.

———. "Versions of the Holocaust: A Review Essay." *Modern Judaism* 3.3 (Oct. 1983).

———. *Writing and Rewriting the Holocaust: Narrative and the Consequences of Interpretation*. Bloomington and Indianapolis: Indiana University Press, 1988.

Index